RICH DAD™

THE BUSINESS OF THE 21ST CENTURY

Other Best-Selling Books in the *Rich Dad* Series

Rich Dad Poor Dad
What the Rich Teach Their Kids About Money That the Poor and Middle Classes Do Not

Rich Dad's CASHFLOW Quadrant
Rich Dad's Guide to Financial Freedom

Rich Dad's Guide to Investing
What the Rich Invest in That the Poor and Middle Classes Do Not

Rich Dad's Rich Kid Smart Kid
Give Your Child a Financial Head-Start

Rich Dad's Retire Young Retire Rich
How to Get Rich Quickly and Stay Rich Forever

Rich Dad's Prophecy
Why the Biggest Stock Market Crash in History Is Still Coming…
and How You Can Prepare Yourself and Profit from It!

Rich Dad's Success Stories
Real-Life Success Stories from Real-Life People Who Followed the Rich Dad Lesson

The Business School
for People Who Like Helping People
The Eight Hidden Values of a Network Marketing Business

Rich Dad's Guide to Becoming Rich Without Cutting Up Your Credit Cards
Turn "Bad Credit" into "Good Credit"

Rich Dad Poor Dad for Teens
The Secrets About Money—That You Don't Learn in School!

Rich Dad's Before You Quit Your Job
10 Real-Life Lessons Every Entrepreneur Should Know About
Building a Multimillion-Dollar Business

Why We Want You to Be Rich
by Robert Kiyosaki and Donald Trump
Provide Insight on How to Improve Your Financial Future

Rich Dad's Increase Your Financial IQ
How to Get Smarter with Your Money

Rich Woman: A Book on Investing for Women
How to Take Charge of Your Money and Your Life

Conspiracy of the Rich: The 8 New Rules of Money
Learn How the Worst of Times Is Actually an Opportunity in the Making!

RICH DAD™

THE BUSINESS OF THE 21ST CENTURY

Robert T. Kiyosaki
With John Fleming and Kim Kiyosaki

DREAM BUILDERS®
An imprint of **Video***Plus*

If you purchase this book without a cover, you should be aware that this book may have been stolen property and reported as "unsold and destroyed" to the publisher. In such case, neither the author nor the publisher has received any payment for this "stripped book."

This publication is designed to provide general information regarding the subject matter covered. However, laws and practices often vary from state to state and are subject to change. Because each factual situation is different, specific advice should be tailored to the particular circumstances. For this reason, the reader is advised to consult with his or her own advisor regarding that individual's specific situation.

The author has taken reasonable precautions in the preparation of this book and believes the facts presented in the book are accurate as of the date it was written. However, neither the author nor the publisher assume any responsibility for any errors or omissions. The author and publisher specifically disclaim any liability resulting from the use or application of the information contained in this book, and the information is not intended to serve as legal, financial, or other professional advice related to individual situations.

Copyright © 2010 by Robert T. Kiyosaki

All rights reserved.

Published by DreamBuilders, an imprint of VideoPlus, L.P., in association with CASHFLOW Technologies, Inc.

CASHFLOW Technologies, Inc.
4330 N. Civic Center Plaza, Suite 100
Scottsdale, Arizona 85251
U.S.A.
800.308.3585
www.richdad.com

CASHFLOW, Rich Dad, Rich Dad's Advisors, Rich Dad's Seminars, ESBI and B-I Triangle are registered trademarks of CASHFLOW Technologies, Inc.

DREAMBUILDERS®

200 Swisher Road
Lake Dallas, Texas 75065
U.S.A.
800.752.2030
Tel: 940.497.9700
www.DreamBuilders.com
www.VideoPlus.com

VideoPlus is a registered trademark of VideoPlus, L.P.

Printed in the United States of America

Designed by DreamBuilders, an imprint of VideoPlus, L.P.

Dedication

I dedicate this book, *The Business of the 21st Century*, to the millions of you who are at a crossroads in life—who are affected by the current economic crisis and feeling helpless as to what you can do to secure your financial future. I want you to know that these are, despite what they may seem, the best times to take control of your future. I have spent my life educating people on how to attain financial freedom, and I know that this book, like the others in my *Rich Dad* series, will provide you with insight needed to create—and sustain—wealth for years to come. Once you learn the truth of how money works and the business opportunities available to you in the 21st century, you will be able to begin building the life you desire.

Contents

Acknowledgments x

Introduction xi

Part One: Take Control of Your Future
1. The Rules Have Changed 3
2. The Silver Lining 9
3. Where Do You Live? 15
4. Your Core Financial Values 19
5. The Mindset of an Entrepreneur 23
6. It's Time to Take Control! 27

Part Two: One Business—Eight Wealth-Building Assets
7. My Years in the Business 33
8. It's Not About Income: It's About Assets That Generate Income 39
9. Asset #1: A Real-World Business Education 43
10. Asset #2: A Profitable Path of Personal Development 49
11. Asset #3: A Circle of Friends Who Share Your Dreams and Values 55
12. Asset #4: The Power of Your Own Network 59
13. Asset #5: A Duplicable, Fully Scalable Business 65
14. Asset #6: Incomparable Leadership Skills 71
15. Asset #7: A Mechanism for Genuine Wealth Creation 77
16. Asset #8: Big Dreams and the Capacity to Live Them 83
17. A Business Where Women Excel 87

Part Three: Your Future Starts Now
18. Choose Wisely 97
19. What It Takes 103
20. Living the Life 111
21. The Business of the 21st Century 115

About the Authors 119

Rich Dad's Resources 122

Acknowledgments

I would like to thank my wife, Kim, for her continued love and support, as well as my Rich Dad family who has helped me get the message of financial education out to millions of people around the globe.

I would also like to thank John Fleming for his invaluable insight on network marketing, and Stuart Johnson, Reed Bilbray, and the staff at VideoPlus for their assistance in putting this book together.

Lastly, I would like to thank John David Mann and J.M. Emmert for bringing their crafts and passions to this project.

Introduction

The economy is in tatters; your job is in trouble—if you still have a job. And you know what? I've been saying it for years.

It took a global financial meltdown for most to hear it. But this book isn't about how or why everything has gone to hell in a handbasket. It's about why this bad news turns out to be very good news—if you know what to do about it.

I learned about business from two people: my father, who was a very well-educated, highly placed government employee, and my best friend's father, who was an eighth-grade dropout and self-made millionaire. My real father suffered financial problems his entire life and died with little to show for all the long years of hard work; my best friend's dad became one of the richest men in Hawaii.

I thought of these two men as my "poor dad" and my "rich dad." I loved and admired my real dad very much, and vowed that I would help as many people as possible avoid suffering the kinds of indignities and failures that plagued his path.

After I left home, I had all kinds of experiences. I served in the Marines as a helicopter pilot in Vietnam. I went to work for Xerox, starting out as their worst salesperson and leaving four years later as their best. After leaving Xerox, I developed several multimillion-dollar international businesses and was able to retire at the age of 47 to pursue my passion—to teach others how to build wealth and live the lives they dream of living, instead of settling for mediocrity and sullen resignation.

In 1997, I wrote about my experiences in a little book. I must have touched a chord with at least a few readers: *Rich Dad Poor Dad* shot to the top of the *New York Times* best-seller list and stayed there for more than four years, and has been described as "the best-selling business book of all time."

Since then, I've put out a whole series of *Rich Dad* books, and although each one has a slightly different focus, they all deliver the exact same message as that first book, and it's the message at the heart of this book you now hold in your hands:

Take responsibility for your finances—or get used to taking orders for the rest of your life. You're either a master of money or a slave to it. Your choice.

Introduction

I was incredibly fortunate in my life to have experiences and mentors that showed me how to build genuine wealth. As a result, I was able to retire completely from any need to work ever again. Up until that time, I was working to build my family's future. Since then, I've been working to help build *yours*.

For the past ten years, I have devoted my life to finding the most effective and practical ways to help people transform their lives in the 21st century by learning how to build genuine wealth. Through our *Rich Dad* books, my partners and I have written about many different types and forms of enterprise and investment. But during these years of intensive research, I have come across one business model in particular that I believe holds the greatest promise for the largest number of people to get control of their financial lives, their futures, and their destinies.

One more thing. When I say *genuine* wealth, I'm not talking about money alone. Money is part of it, but it's not the whole. Building genuine wealth is as much about the *builder* as it is about the *built*.

In this book, I'm going to show you why you need to build your own business, and exactly what kind of business. But this isn't just about changing the type of business you're working with; it's also about changing you. I can show you how to find what you need to grow the perfect business for you, but for your business to grow, you will have to grow as well.

Welcome to the business of the 21st century.

PART ONE

Take Control of Your Future

*Why you need to have
a business of your own*

Chapter 1

The Rules Have Changed

We live in troubled times. The last few years have brought us a steady parade of fear and panic in the headlines, boardrooms, and kitchen tables across America. Globalization, outsourcing, downsizing, foreclosures, subprime mortgages and credit default swaps, ponzi schemes, Wall Street fiascoes, recession ... it's just one piece of bad news after another.

During the first few months of 2009, U.S. company layoffs reached about a quarter-million per month. As I write this in late 2009, unemployment is at 10.2 percent and still rising, and underemployment (where your job stays in place but your hours and pay are drastically cut back) is even worse. The rampant decline in gainful employment is a ravaging epidemic to which few are immune. From executives and middle managers to administration employees and blue-collar workers, from bankers to retail clerks, all are at risk. Even the healthcare industry, until recently considered a job-safe zone, is trimming away significant chunks of its workforce.

In a 2009 *USA Today* survey, 60 percent of Americans polled said they see today's economic situation as the biggest crisis in their lifetime.

In the fall of 2008, a lot of people's retirement portfolios suddenly lost half their value—or more. Real estate crashed. What people *thought* were their solid, reliable assets turned out to be about as solid as water vapor. Job security is gone, a thing of the past. In a 2009 *USA Today* survey, 60 percent of Americans polled said they see today's economic situation as the biggest crisis in their lifetime.

Of course, you already know all this. But here's what you may not know: *None of this is really news.* Sure, it took a major economic crisis for people to start waking up to the fact that their livelihoods were at risk. But your income didn't become at risk overnight—it was *always* at risk.

Most of the U.S. population has been living for years on the knife-edge precipice between solvency and ruin, relying on the next paycheck or two to meet each

CHAPTER 1: The Rules Have Changed

month's expenses, typically with only a very thin cushion of cash savings—or more often, no cushion at all. That paycheck is called "trading your time for money," and during a recession, it is the *least* reliable source of income there is. Why? Because when the number of employed people starts dropping, there is less disposable income in circulation to pay for your time.

I Told You So

Not to be an I-told-you-so, but ... *I told you so.*

I've been saying this for years: There is no longer such a thing as a safe and secure job. Corporate America is a 20th-century dinosaur, trembling on the edge of extinction, and the only way for you to have a genuinely secure future is for you to take control of that future.

Here's what I wrote in 2001, in a book titled *The Business School for People Who Like Helping People*:

> *In my opinion, the United States and many Western nations have a financial disaster coming, caused by our educational system's failure to adequately provide a realistic financial education program for students.*

That same year, in an interview for Nightingale-Conant, I said:

> *If you think mutual funds are going to be there for you, if you want to bet your life on the ups and downs of the stock market, that's your retirement you're betting on. What happens if the stock market goes up and then comes crashing down again when you're 85 years old? You have no control. I'm not saying mutual funds are bad. I'm just saying they're not safe and they're not smart, and I wouldn't bet my financial future on them.*
>
> *Never before in the history of the world have so many people bet their retirement on the stock market. That is insane. Do you think Social Security is going to be there to take care of you? Then you also believe in the Easter Bunny.*

And in an interview I did in March 2005, I said this:

> *The No. 1 strength of a paper asset is its liquidity—and that is also its No. 1 weakness. We all know there's going to be another market crash and we're going to be wiped out again. Why would you do that?*

So what just happened? There was another market crash and many people got wiped out again. Why? Because our habits and mindset caught up with us.

In 1971, the American economy went off the gold standard. This happened without the approval of Congress, by the way, but the important thing is that it happened. Why is that significant? Because it cleared the way for us to start printing more and more money, as much as we liked, without it being tied to any actual, hard, real value.

This shift away from reality opened the gates for the biggest economic boom in history. Over the next three and a half decades, the American middle class exploded. As the dollar devalued and the on-the-books value of real estate and other assets inflated, ordinary people became millionaires. Suddenly credit was available to anyone, anytime, anywhere, and credit cards began popping up like mushrooms after a spring rain. To pay off those credit cards, Americans started using their homes as ATMs, refinancing and borrowing, borrowing and refinancing.

After all, real estate always keeps going *up* in value, right?

Wrong. By 2007 we had pumped as much hot air into this financial balloon as it could take—and the fantasy came crashing down to earth again. And it wasn't just Lehman Brothers and Bear Stearns that collapsed. Millions lost their 401(k)s, their pensions, and their jobs.

The number of people living officially below the poverty line is rising rapidly. The number of people who are working beyond the age of 65 is increasing.

In the 1950s, when General Motors was the most powerful corporation in America, the press picked up a statement by GM's president and turned it into a slogan that carried for decades: "As GM goes, so goes the nation." Well, folks, that may not be all good news, because where GM went in 2009 was into bankruptcy, and by that same summer, the state of California was paying its bills with IOUs instead of cash.

Right now, the percentage of Americans who own their homes is dropping. Mortgage foreclosures are at an all-time high. The number of middle-class families is dropping. Savings accounts are smaller, if they exist at all, and family debt is greater. The number of people living officially below the poverty line is rising rapidly. The number of people who are working beyond the age of 65 is increasing. The number of new bankruptcies is going through the roof. And many Americans do not have enough to retire—not even close.

Has all this bad news got your attention? Sure it has, and you're not alone. Americans everywhere have finally stopped rolling over and hitting the Snooze button. Great! Now you're awake to what's going on, and it isn't pretty. So let's take a deeper look and see what it really means—and what there is you can do about it.

It's a New Century

When I was a kid, my parents taught me the same formula for success that you probably learned: Go to school, study hard, and get good grades so you can get a secure, high-paying job with benefits—and your job will take care of you.

CHAPTER 1: The Rules Have Changed

But that's Industrial-Age thinking, and we're not in the Industrial Age anymore. Your job is *not* going to take care of you. The government will *not* take care of you. *Nobody's* going to take care of you. It's a new century, and the rules have changed.

My parents believed in job security, company pensions, Social Security, and Medicare. These are all worn-out, obsolete ideas left over from an age gone by. Today job security is a joke, and the very idea of lifetime employment with a single company—an ideal so proudly championed by IBM in its heyday—is as anachronistic as a manual typewriter.

Many thought their 401(k) retirement plans were safe. Hey, they were backed by blue-chip stocks and mutual funds, what could go wrong? As it turned out, *everything* could go wrong. The reason these once-sacred cows no longer give any milk is that they are *all* obsolete: pensions, job security, retirement security—it's all Industrial-Age thinking. We're in the Information Age now, and we need to use Information-Age thinking.

Fortunately, people are starting to listen and learn. It's a shame that it takes suffering and hardship to bring the lesson home, but at least the lessons *are* hitting home. Every time we experience a major crisis—the dot-com bust, the economic aftermath of 9/11, the financial panic of '08, and recession of '09—more people realize that the old safety nets just won't hold up anymore.

The corporate myth is over. If you've spent years climbing the corporate ladder, have you ever stopped to notice the view? What view, you ask? The rear end of the person in front of you. That's what you get to look forward to. If that's the way you want to view the rest of your life, then this book probably isn't for you. But if you are sick and tired of looking at someone else's behind, then read on.

Don't Be Fooled Again

As I write this, unemployment is still on the rise. By the time you *read* these words, who knows? The situation may have changed. Don't be fooled. When employment and real estate values turn around and credit loosens up again, as they inevitably will, don't be lulled into that same-old sense of false security that got you and the rest of the world into this mess in the first place.

In the summer of 2008, gas prices were soaring over $4 a gallon. SUV sales sank like a stone, and suddenly everyone was on the small-car-and-hybrid bandwagon. But look what happened next. By 2009, gas prices had fallen back down below $2—and so help me, people started buying SUVs again!

What?! Do we *really* think fuel prices are going to stay nice and low? That gas prices are down for good now, and therefore gas-guzzlers make perfect sense to buy? Can we really be that shortsighted? (I'm trying to be nice here. The word I was *going* to use was "stupid.")

Unfortunately, the answer is yes. We aren't just fooled once; we let ourselves be fooled over and over again. We all grew up hearing the fable of the ant and the grasshopper, but the overwhelming majority of us keep living with the foresight of a grasshopper anyway.

Don't be distracted by the headlines. There is always some idiotic buzz going on that tries to pull your attention away from the serious business of building your life. It's just noise. Whether it's terrorism, recession, or the latest election-cycle scandals, it's got nothing to do with what you need to be doing today to build your future.

During the Great Depression, there were people who made fortunes. And during the greatest boom times, like the real estate surge of the '80s, there were millions and millions of people who neglected to take charge of their future—who ignored everything I'm going to share with you in this book—and ended up struggling or broke. Most of them, in fact, are still struggling or broke today.

The economy is not the issue. The issue is *you*.

Are you angry at the corruption in the corporate world? At Wall Street and the big banks that let this happen? At the government for not doing enough, or for doing too much, or for doing too much of the wrong things and not enough of the right things? Are you angry at yourself for not taking control sooner?

Life is tough. The question is, what are you going to do about it? Moaning and groaning won't secure your future. Neither will blaming Wall Street, the big bankers, corporate America, or the government.

If you want a solid future, you need to create it. You can take charge of your future *only* when you take control of your *income source*. You need your own business.

CHAPTER 2

The Silver Lining

On July 13, 2009, *TIME* magazine ran a piece on page 2 they called "10 Questions for Robert Kiyosaki." One of the questions asked of me was this: "Are there opportunities to create new companies in this turbulent economy?"

"Are you kidding?!" was my first thought. Here is how I answered:

> *This is the best time. When times are bad is when the real entrepreneurs emerge. Entrepreneurs don't really care if the market's up or down. They're creating better products and better processes. So when somebody says, "Oh, there's less opportunity now," it's because they're losers.*

You've heard an awful lot of bad news about the economy. Ready for the good news? Actually, the bad news *is* the good news. I'll tell you the same thing I told *TIME* magazine: *A recession is the best time to start your own business.* When the economy slows down, entrepreneurialism heats up like a stoked-up wood stove on a cold winter night.

> *Q: What do the Microsoft and Disney empires have in common, besides the fact that they are both hugely successful billion-dollar businesses that have become household names?*
>
> *A: They were both launched during a recession.*

In fact, more than half the corporations that make up the Dow Jones Industrial Average got their starts during a recession.

Why? Simple: In times of economic uncertainty, *people get creative.* They break out of their comfort zones and take initiative to help make ends meet. It's a matter of good, old-fashioned American entrepreneurialism at its best. When the going gets tough, the tough get going.

For one thing, the market for new opportunity is ripe during tough economic times. Five years ago, when housing values were soaring and credit was available

CHAPTER 2: The Silver Lining

everywhere, nobody was hungry. People's bellies were full, they felt safe, and few were looking for any alternative means of income. Employees weren't worried about the financial stability of their employers or whether a pink slip might be in their future.

But now that layoffs are rampant and everyone is worried about what the future holds, millions of people are soberly reevaluating their finances and realizing that if they want to have a secure future they can count on, they're going to have to come up with a Plan B. People today are hungrier than ever to earn extra money, and because of that, they are more receptive and more inclined to open their minds to new avenues.

In fact, this was true even *before* the recent economic meltdown. Ever since the '80s, and especially since the turn of the century, the drive to control our own economic futures has been building. Here's what the U.S. Chamber of Commerce said in a 2007 report titled *Work, Entrepreneurship and Opportunity in 21st Century America:* "Millions of Americans are embracing entrepreneurship by running their own small businesses."

72 percent of all adult Americans would rather work for themselves than for a job, and 67 percent think about quitting their jobs "regularly" or "constantly."

Now, I'm no economist, but I know someone who is: Paul Zane Pilzer.

Paul is a whiz kid, was Citibank's youngest-ever vice president, and left the banking world to make millions going into business for himself. He's had a few *New York Times* best-sellers, predicted the Savings & Loan crisis before it happened, and served as an economic advisor in two presidential administrations. He's someone worth listening to.

Paul talks about a 180-degree shift in cultural values around the nature of career paths, with the conventional corporate-employee career structure giving way to the entrepreneurial path.

"The traditional wisdom in the second half of the 20th century," says Paul, "was to go to school, get a good education, and go to work for a large company. The idea of going into business for yourself was most often regarded as risky. Admirable, perhaps, but risky ... and maybe a little crazy. Today it's completely the other way around."

Paul's right. That U.S. Chamber of Commerce report I mentioned also refers to a Gallup poll finding that 61 percent of Americans say they would prefer to be their own boss. Another poll, this one by the Fresno research firm Decipher, found that 72 percent of all adult Americans would rather work for themselves than for a job, and 67 percent think about quitting their jobs "regularly" or "constantly."

And it's not just about *making* a living; it's also about the quality of *how* we're living. People are waking up to the fact that they want more control over their lives. They want to be more connected to their families, be in charge of their own time, work from their homes, determine their own destinies. In that Decipher study, 84 percent of respondents said they would be more passionate about their work if they owned their own business. The No. 1 reason they gave for wanting to work for themselves? "To be more passionate about my work life."

What's happening is that the 20th-century myth of job security, with its promise that the path to a long, happy, fulfilling life is to find a job working for someone else, is crumbling before our eyes.

The Employment Mythology

Most of us are so brainwashed by our circumstances that we think of employment as normal. But far from being historically "normal," the whole concept of being an employee is actually a fairly recent phenomenon.

During the Agrarian Age, most people were entrepreneurs. Yes, they were farmers who worked the king's lands, but they were not the king's employees. They didn't receive a paycheck from the king. In fact, it was the other way around: The farmer paid the king a tax for the right to use his land. These farmers actually made their living as small-business entrepreneurs. They were butchers, bakers, and candlestick makers who passed on their trade through the family lineage in what have come down to us as common last names: Smith, for the village blacksmith; Baker, for bakery owners; Farmer, because their family's business was farming; Taylor, derived from the tailor's profession; and Cooper, the old term for the barrel-maker's trade.

It was not until the Industrial Age that a new demand began growing: the demand for employees. In response, the government took over the task of mass education, adopting the Prussian system, which is what most Western school systems in the world are still modeled after today.

Have you ever wondered where the idea of retirement at age 65 came from? I'll tell you where: Otto von Bismarck, the president of Prussia, in 1889. Actually, Bismarck's plan kicked in at age 70, not 65, but it hardly matters. Promising their old folks a guaranteed pension after age 65 was not much of an economic risk for Bismarck's government: At the time, the life expectancy of the average Prussian was about 45. Today, so many are living well into their 80s and 90s that the same promise might well bankrupt the federal government within the next generation.

When you research the philosophy behind Prussian education, you will find that the purpose was to produce soldiers and employees, people who would follow orders and do as they were told. The Prussian system is for mass-producing employees.

In America in the '60s and '70s, companies like IBM made "employment for life" the gold standard of job security. But employment at IBM hit its peak in 1985, and the whole concept of the solid, reliable corporate career has been in decline ever since.

CHAPTER 2: The Silver Lining

"As GM goes, so goes the nation…"

Here we are, half a century later, and things aren't going so well for GM. Does that mean America is doomed? No, but here's what is doomed: the myth of corporate security and the forty-year plan.

Entrepreneurial Fever

I'm not saying employment is a bad thing. I'm just saying it's only one way of generating income, and one that is extremely limited. What's happening right now is that people are waking up to this fact. These people—including you—are realizing that the only way they're going to have what they really want in life is by setting foot on the path of the entrepreneur.

And by the way, I'm not the only one who sees this. You may or may not have heard of Muhammad Yunus, author of *Banker to the Poor*, but the Nobel Committee in Oslo, Norway, has heard of him. They gave him the Nobel Peace Prize in 2006 for his concept of microcredit for Third World entrepreneurs. "All people are entrepreneurs," says Yunus, "but many don't have the opportunity to find that out."

> **Entrepreneurial fever has been kicking into high gear, because when the economy slows down, entrepreneurial activity heats up. In fact, entrepreneurs *flourish* in down times.**

He said that *before* the economy started tanking in '07 and '08, and in the wake of all the financial bad news, more and more people are actively seeking the opportunity to do exactly what Mr. Yunus is talking about.

Entrepreneurial fever has been kicking into high gear, because when the economy slows down, entrepreneurial activity heats up. In fact, entrepreneurs *flourish* in down times. In times of uncertainty, we look for other ways to generate income. When we know we can't rely on employers, we begin to look to ourselves. We start thinking maybe it's time to break out of our comfort zones and get creative to help make ends meet.

A U.S. Federal Reserve survey shows that the average household net worth for entrepreneurs is five times that of conventional employees. That means entrepreneurs are five times more likely to come out of this downturn unscathed and even stronger than before, because they've created *their own strong economy*.

A recent survey found that most U.S. voters view entrepreneurship as the key to solving the current economic crisis. "History has repeatedly demonstrated that new companies and entrepreneurship are the way to bolster a flagging economy," said the survey's executive director.

No kidding.

Maybe those "most U.S. voters" who say they believe that will actually get off their duffs and *do* something about it. It's possible, though I'm not holding my breath. But right now, the flagging economy that I'm most interested in seeing bolstered by entrepreneurship is *yours*.

These may be economic hard times for the majority, but for some entrepreneurs—the ones who are open-minded enough to understand what I'm going to explain in the next few chapters—these are times pregnant with economic potential. Not only is now the time to have your own business, but in fact, there has never been a better time than right now, today.

As I said, when the going gets tough, the tough get going. And if that's true—which it is—then that leaves just two questions.

First: Are you willing to be tough?

And if your answer is "yes," then question No. 2 is, Get going doing *what?*

I can't answer that first question for you, but I know *exactly* how to answer the second one. Answering that question is what this book is all about.

CHAPTER 3

Where Do You Live?

So you've been working hard for years, climbing the ladder. Maybe you're still near the bottom of the ladder, or maybe you even got near the top. Where you are on the ladder doesn't really matter. What matters is the question that you may have forgotten to stop and ask before putting in all that time and effort climbing: Where is this ladder planted?

As Stephen R. Covey points out, it doesn't matter how fast or high you climb on the ladder if it's leaning against the wrong wall.

The purpose of this chapter is for you to stop climbing for a minute and see where your ladder is planted. And, if you're not happy where it is, to find out where you might want to move it.

How Do You Make the Money You Make?

Most people assume that their financial standing is defined by how much they earn, how much they're worth, or some combination of both. And there's no doubt that this has some bearing. *Forbes* magazine defines "rich" as a person who earns in excess of $1 million per year (about $83,333 per month, or just under $20,000 a week), and "poor" as someone who earns less than $25,000 a year.

But even more important than the quantity of money you make is the *quality* of money you make. In other words, not just how much you make, but how you make it—where it comes from. There are actually *four distinct sources* of cashflow. Each is quite different from the other, and each defines and determines a very different lifestyle, regardless of the amount of cash you earn.

After publishing *Rich Dad Poor Dad,* I wrote a book to explain these four different income worlds. Many people have said that this book, *Cashflow Quadrant,* is the most important writing I've done because it goes right to the heart of the crucial issues involved for people who are ready to make true changes in their lives.

CHAPTER 3: Where Do You Live?

The *cashflow quadrant* represents the different methods by which a cash income is generated. For example, an *employee* earns money by holding a job and working for someone else or a company. The *self-employed* are people who earn money working for themselves, either as solo operators or through their own small business. A *business owner* owns a large business (typically defined as 500 employees or more) that generates money. *Investors* earn money from their various investments—in other words, money generating more money.

E = **E**mployee
S = **S**elf-employed or Small-business owner
B = **B**usiness owner
I = **I**nvestor

Which quadrant do you live in? In other words, from which quadrant do you receive the majority of the income on which you live?

The E Quadrant

The overwhelming majority of us learn, live, love, and leave this life entirely within the E quadrant. Our educational system and culture train us, from the cradle to the grave, in how to live in the world of the E quadrant.

The operating philosophy for this world is what my poor dad—my real father—taught me, and what you probably learned, too, when you were growing up: Go to school, study hard and get good grades, and get a good job with benefits at a great company.

The S Quadrant

Driven by the urge for more freedom and self-determination, a lot of people migrate from the E quadrant to the S quadrant. This is the place where people go to "strike out on their own" and pursue the American Dream.

The S quadrant includes a huge range of earning power, all the way from the teenage freelance baby sitter or landscaper just starting out in life to the highly paid private-practice lawyer, consultant, or public speaker.

But whether you're earning $8 an hour or $80,000 a year, the S quadrant is typically a trap. You may have thought you were "firing your boss," but what really happened is that you just changed bosses. You are still an employee. The only difference is that when you want to blame your boss for your problems, that boss is you.

The S quadrant can be a thankless and difficult place to live. Everyone picks on you here. The government picks on you—you spend one full day a week just in tax compliance. Your employees pick on you, your customers pick on you, and your family picks on you because you never take any time off. How can you? If you do, you lose ground. You have no free time because if you take time off, the business doesn't earn money.

In a very real way, the S stands for slavery: You don't really own your business; your business owns you.

The B Quadrant

The B quadrant is where people go to create big businesses. The difference between an S business and a B business is that you work for your S business, but your B business works *for you*.

I have many B businesses, including my manufacturing business, my real estate business, mining companies, and others.

Those who live and work in the B quadrant make themselves recession-proof, because they control the source of their own income.

The I Quadrant

This is not rocket science. My rich dad taught me to live in the I quadrant by playing Monopoly, and we all know how that works: four green houses, one red hotel; four green houses, one red hotel.

Changing Jobs Is Not Changing Quadrants

Now let me explain why it's so important to understand these different quadrants. How often have you heard someone complain about their job, then decide to make a change, only to end up a few years later with the same old complaints?

> *I keep working harder and harder, but I'm just not getting ahead.*
>
> *Every time I get a raise, it gets eaten up by taxes and higher expenses.*
>
> *I'd rather be doing [fill in the blank], but I can't afford to go back to school and learn a whole-new profession at this stage of my life.*
>
> *This job stinks! My boss stinks! Life stinks! (etc.)*

These and dozens of others like them are all statements that reveal a person who is trapped—trapped not in a certain job, but in an entire quadrant. The problem is, most of the time when people do get up the initiative to actually make a change in their lives, all they do is change jobs. What they need to do is change *quadrants*.

Breaking away from those typical job structures and creating your own stream of income puts you in the best position to weather an economic storm, simply because you are no longer dependent on a boss or on the economy to determine your annual income. Now *you* determine it.

The left-hand side—the E and S quadrants—is where most people live. That's where we are brought up and trained to live. "Get good grades, so you can get a good job," we're told. But your grades don't matter in the B quadrant. Your banker doesn't ask to see your report card; he wants to see your financial statement.

Breaking away from those typical job structures and creating your own stream of income puts you in the best position to weather an economic storm, simply because you are no longer dependent on a boss or on the economy to determine your annual income. Now *you* determine it.

At least 80 percent of the population lives in the left-hand side of this picture. The E quadrant, especially, is where we are taught we will find safety and security. On the other hand, the right-hand side—the B and I quadrants—is where freedom resides. If you want to live on that side, then you can make it happen. But if you want the relative safety of the left-hand side, then maybe what I have to share here is not for you. That's a decision only you can make.

Which quadrant do you live in?

Which quadrant do you *want* to live in?

CHAPTER 4

Your Core Financial Values

The four quadrants are not just four different business structures. It's even more about four different *mindsets*. Which quadrant you choose to earn your primary income from has less to do with external circumstances—your education, training, the economy, what appear to be the available opportunities around you—and much more to do with who you are at your core: your strengths, weaknesses, and central interests.

It is a matter of your *core financial values*. It is these core differences that attract us to or repel us from the different quadrants.

This is important to grasp because it means that shifting from the E or S quadrant over to the B quadrant isn't as simple as filling out a change-of-address form at the post office. You not only change what you do, but in a very real way, you also change *who you are*. Or at least, *how you think*.

Some people may love being employees, while others hate it. Some people love owning companies, but do not want to run them. Certain people love investing, while others see only the risk of losing money. Most of us are a little of each of these characters. It is also important to note that you can be rich or poor in all of the four quadrants. There are people who earn millions and people who go bankrupt in each of the quadrants. Living in any one quadrant does not in itself necessarily guarantee financial success.

You can tell which quadrant people are living in by listening to their words. When I was 9 years old, I began sitting in with my rich dad when he interviewed people for possible hiring. From these interviews, I learned to listen for people's core values—values that my rich dad said came from their souls.

Here are some key phrases that emerge from each quadrant, along with a snapshot of the core values of each.

B wealth-building
security E
financial freedom
independence S I

E Quadrant Values

"I am looking for a safe, secure job with good pay and excellent benefits."

For someone living in the E quadrant, the core value is *security*.

You might be the top-earning vice president of a company yet still share the same core values as the company's janitor, who earns a tenth of your salary. A person in the E quadrant, regardless if he is the janitor or the president, often thinks or says words such as, "I am looking for a safe, secure job with benefits." Or, "How much do we get for overtime?" Or, "How many paid holidays do we have?"

When I'm having a conversation with someone in the E quadrant and I talk about how much I love starting my own businesses, he may say, "Yeah, but isn't that risky?" We each see life from our own core values. What is exciting for me is frightening to someone else. This is why, when I'm in the company of people who live in the E and S quadrants, I usually talk about the weather, sports, or what is on television.

S Quadrant Values

"If you want something done right, do it yourself."

For people in the S quadrant, the core value is *independence*. They want the freedom to do what they want. When a person says, "I'm going to quit my job and go out on my own," the path taken is from the E quadrant to the S quadrant.

People found in the S quadrant are small-business owners, mom and pop businesses, specialists, and consultants. For example, I have a friend who installs big-screen televisions, phone systems, and security systems in rich people's homes. He has a staff of three and is happy to be the boss of just three people. He is a hard-core, hardworking S. Commissioned salespeople, such as real estate agents and insurance brokers, are in the S quadrant. The S quadrant is also filled with professional people, such as doctors, lawyers, and accountants who do not belong to a large medical, legal, or accounting firm.

People living in the S quadrant often take great pride in the work of their own hands or brains. If they had a theme song, it would be either, "Nobody Does It Better" or "My Way." Yet, behind the façade of independence, you will often find a lack of trust at the core of this person's approach to business—which also means his approach to life, because how we view our business tends to be how we view *everything*.

An S is often paid by commission or by the amount of time spent on a job. For example, an S may be heard saying words such as, "My commission is 6 percent of the total purchase price." Or, "I charge $100 an hour." Or, "My fee is cost plus 10 percent."

Whenever I meet someone from the E or S quadrant who is having difficulty making the transition to the B quadrant, I usually see a person with great technical or management skills but little leadership ability. My rich dad used to say, "If you're the leader of the team and you're also the smartest person on the team, your team is in trouble." People in the S quadrant often don't work too well with teams; they may even have a bit of an ego problem.

To make the jump from S to B quadrant, what is needed is a quantum jump not in technical skills, but in leadership skills. As I've said many times before, in the real world, the A students often go to work for the C students—and the B students work for the government.

If you've ever heard yourself saying, "If you want something done right, do it yourself," or if you tend to think that way, it might be a good time to take a good long look at that philosophy.

B Quadrant Values

"I'm looking for the best people to join my team."

For people in the B quadrant, the core value is *wealth-building*.

People who start from nothing and build great B quadrant businesses are often people with powerful life missions, who value a great team and efficient teamwork and want to serve and work with as many people as possible.

While a person in the S quadrant wants to be the best in his or her field, a B quadrant person wants to build a team out of other people who are the best in *their* fields. Henry Ford surrounded himself with people smarter than he was. While an S quadrant businessperson is often the smartest or most talented person in the room, this is often not true for a B quadrant businessperson.

When you own a B quadrant business, you will often deal with people who are much smarter, more experienced, and more capable than you are. My rich dad had no formal education, but I watched him deal with bankers, lawyers, accountants, investment advisors, and experts, many of whom had advanced degrees. In raising money for his businesses, he often dealt with people who were far richer than he was. If he had lived by the motto, "If you want something done right, do it yourself," he would have ended up a complete failure.

When it comes to being paid, a true B quadrant person can leave his or her business and still get paid. In most cases, if someone in the S quadrant stops working, the income stops also. Therefore, a question you may want to ask yourself now is, "If I stop working today, how much income continues to come in?" If your income stops in six months or less, then, chances are, you are in the E or S quadrants. A person in the B or I quadrants can stop working for years and the money will continue to come in.

I Quadrant Values

"What's my return on investment?"

What people in the I quadrant value most is *financial freedom*. The investor loves the idea of his money working instead of him working.

Investors invest in many things. They may invest in gold coins, real estate, businesses, or paper assets such as stocks, bonds, and mutual funds.

If your income comes from company or government retirement plans, rather than your own personal investing knowledge, then that is income from the E

CHAPTER 4: Your Core Financial Values

quadrant. In other words, your boss or the business is still paying its bill for your years of service.

Words an investor might be heard saying are, "I'm receiving a 20 percent return on my assets," or, "Show me the company's financials," or, "How much deferred maintenance is on the property?"

Different Quadrants, Different Investors

In today's world, we all need to be investors. However, our school systems do not teach us much about investing. Oh, I know that some schools teach stock picking, but to me, that is not investing; that's gambling.

Years ago, my rich dad pointed out to me that most employees invest in mutual funds or savings. He also said, "Just because you're successful in one quadrant, such as the E, S, or B, does not mean you will be successful in the I quadrant. Doctors are often the worst investors."

My rich dad also pointed out to me that different quadrants invest in different ways. For example, a person in the S quadrant might be heard saying, "I don't

---

If you want to get rich, *you're going to have to move*. You don't need a new job; you need a *new address*.

---

invest in real estate because I don't want to fix toilets." A person in the B quadrant addressing the same investment challenge might say, "I want to hire a good property-management company to fix my toilets at night." In other words, an S quadrant investor will think he has to do the property maintenance on his own, and a B quadrant investor will hire another company to do the property maintenance for him. Different people, different mindsets; different quadrants, different values.

By now, you've probably figured out where I'm going with this. It comes down to a pretty simple thing: If you want to get rich, *you're going to have to move*. You don't need a new job; you need a *new address*.

If you want control over your life and destiny, if you want real freedom—the freedom to call your shots, set your schedule, spend time with your family and with yourself, doing the things you love to do—if you want to live the life you were designed to live—no holds barred, a life of passion and excitement and fulfillment—in short, if you want to *be rich* and *live rich*, then it's time to pack up your stuff and move.

It's time to leave the left side of the chart and move over to the B and I quadrants.

CHAPTER 5

The Mindset of an Entrepreneur

After finishing college, I enrolled in a traditional business school to pursue my MBA so I could be a trained and educated entrepreneur. I lasted nine months before dropping out. Needless to say, I did not receive my MBA upon leaving.

These days, business schools often invite me to come speak to their students in classes on entrepreneurship. I probably don't need to point out that I sometimes find this ironic.

Common questions these students ask me are, "How do I find investors?" and "How do I raise capital?" I understand the questions, because they haunted me when I left the security of a traditional job and became an entrepreneur myself. I had no money, and no one wanted to invest with me. The big venture-capital firms were not knocking on my door.

So what do I tell these business-school students? I tell them, "You just do it. You do it because you *have* to do it. If you don't, you are out of business.

You do *not* have to raise the capital to create your business, because that has already been done for you. But you do have to build your business!

"Today, even though I have enough money, all I do is raise capital. For an entrepreneur, that is Job No. 1. We raise capital from three groups of people: customers, investors, and employees. Your job as an entrepreneur is to get your customers to buy your products. If you can get customers to give you money by buying your products, your investors will give you lots of money. And if you have employees, your job is to get them to produce and make you at least ten times more money than you pay them. If you can't get your employees to produce at least ten times more than you pay them, you're out of business, and if you're out of business, you don't need to raise any more money."

CHAPTER 5: The Mindset of an Entrepreneur

This is *not* the answer most MBA students are looking for. Most are looking for the magic formula, the secret recipe, the quick business plan to riches. This doesn't seem to be the answer their instructors are hoping I'll give, either, because I notice them squirming when I say this stuff. Why? Because while they *teach* entrepreneurship, most of them are not themselves entrepreneurs, which is why they have a steady teaching job with a steady paycheck and are hoping for tenure.

My point is not that you have to raise money. In fact, in the business model I'm going to share with you in this book, you do *not* have to raise the capital to create your business, because that has already been done for you. But you do have to build your business!

My point is that this is what defines an entrepreneur: *You make things happen.* You pull yourself out of the rows of passenger seats, walk to the head of the bus, and get behind the wheel of your life.

What Does It Take to Be an Entrepreneur?

Entrepreneurs are the richest people on earth. We know the names of the famous entrepreneurs: Richard Branson and Donald Trump, Oprah Winfrey and Steve Jobs, Rupert Murdoch and Ted Turner. But most wealthy entrepreneurs are people you and I will never hear of, because they don't command media attention; they just quietly live rich lives.

I often hear people debate the question, "Are entrepreneurs born or can they be developed?" Some think it takes a special person or a certain magic to be an entrepreneur. To me, being an entrepreneur is not that big a deal; you just do it.

Let me give you an example. There's a teenager in my neighborhood who has a thriving baby-sitting business and hires her junior-high classmates to work for her. She is an entrepreneur. Another young boy has a handyman business after school. He is an entrepreneur. Most kids have no fear, while for most adults, that's all they *do* have.

It takes courage to discover, develop and donate your genius to the world.

Today, there are millions of people who dream of quitting their jobs and becoming entrepreneurs, running their own businesses. The problem is, for most people, their dream is just a dream. So the question is, why do so many fail to go for their dream of becoming an entrepreneur?

I have a friend who is a brilliant hairstylist. When it comes to making women look beautiful, he is a magician. For years, he's talked about opening his own salon. He has big plans, but sadly, he still remains small, running a single chair in a large salon, constantly at odds with the owner.

Another friend has a wife who became tired of being a flight attendant. Two years ago, she quit her job and went to school to become a hairstylist. A month ago, she had a grand opening for her salon. It is a spectacular environment and she has attracted some of the best hairstylists to work there.

When the first friend heard about her salon, he said, "How can she open a salon? She has no talent. She is not gifted. She wasn't trained in New York like I was. And besides, she doesn't have any experience. I give her a year and she's going to fail."

Maybe she will fail: Statistics show that 90 percent of all businesses fail in the first five years. On the other hand, maybe she won't. The point is that she's doing it. She has grasped the impact that courage has in shaping our lives. *It takes courage to discover, develop and donate your genius to the world.*

Of U.S. lottery winners who win in excess of $3 million each, 80 percent are bankrupt within three years. Why? Because money alone does not make you rich. These people may add numbers to their checking accounts, but the mere numbers do not make them rich, because they do not change how they think.

Your mind is *infinite*. It's your doubts that are limiting. Ayn Rand, the author of *Atlas Shrugged*, said, "Wealth is the product of man's capacity to think." So if you are ready to change your life, I'm going to introduce you to an environment that will allow your brain to think—and you to grow richer.

What Do You Want to Be When You Grow Up?

When I was a kid, my real dad often told me go to school and get good grades so I could get a safe, secure job. He was programming me for the E quadrant. My mother would urge me to consider becoming a doctor or lawyer. "That way you'll always have a profession to fall back on." She was programming me for the S quadrant. My rich dad told me that if I wanted to grow up to become rich, I should become a business owner and an investor. He was programming me for the B and I quadrants.

When I returned from Vietnam, I had to make up my mind which advice I would listen to. You are faced with the same choice.

One reason you want to create your own business is to get your dignity back.

Don't underestimate the importance of this reason. The world is full of bullies and small-minded people, and whether they are your boss, your manager, your neighbor, or even your friend, you don't want them pushing you around anymore. You want to take control of your life. You want to have the courage not to care when other people bully you around; you want to have the freedom to think and act for yourself.

A Maserati Mind

Now let's ask that question again: *Where do you live?* Now you can appreciate what shifting from one cashflow quadrant to another means. It's not just a different structure. It's a different approach to life.

Yes, it's about the business, but at the same time, it's not really about the business—that's only the external form. Putting a horse farmer behind the wheel of

CHAPTER 5: The Mindset of an Entrepreneur

a Maserati doesn't make him a racing car driver. He needs the skills, the training, and, most important, the *mindset* of a racing car driver.

The same is true of your financial life. You need to adopt the mindset of an entrepreneur. That mindset comes down to this: An entrepreneur is self-determining.

One of the beauties of the *business of the 21st century* is that all the groundwork of the business is already done for you.

You make things happen, which means you don't get to blame *anyone* or *anything* outside yourself.

Not that you're going to have to do it all yourself from the ground up, like I did with my businesses. No, one of the beauties of *the business of the 21st century* is that all the groundwork of the business is already done for you—and you get to have experienced leaders committed to your success to guide you.

But make no mistake: If it's going to happen for you, you are going to be the one who makes it happen. And for *that* to happen, you need to have the mindset of an entrepreneur. If you don't, then no matter how good the business is or how great your teachers are, the business is going to have a tough time getting results.

The business model we'll explore in Part Two of this book is a Maserati, but you are the one behind the wheel. First and foremost, *it's about you*. Are you prepared to take the wheel? Do you have what it takes?

CHAPTER 6

It's Time to Take Control!

It was 1985 and my wife, Kim, and I were homeless. We were unemployed and had little money left from savings; our credit cards were exhausted and we lived in an old brown Toyota with reclining seats that served as beds. At the end of a week of sleeping in our car, the harsh reality of who we were, what we were doing, and where we were headed began to sink in.

After a friend realized our desperate situation, she offered us a room in her basement. When friends and family were informed of our plight, the first question was always, "Why don't you just get a job?" At first we attempted to explain, but we had a hard time clarifying our reasons to our well-meaning inquisitors. When you're talking to someone who values having a job, it is difficult to explain why you might not want a job.

We occasionally earned a few dollars doing a few odd jobs here and there. But we did that only to keep food in our stomachs and gas in our house—I mean, our car.

I must admit that during moments of deep personal doubt, the idea of a safe, secure job with a paycheck was appealing. But because job security was not what we were looking for, we kept pushing on, living day to day on the brink of the financial abyss. We knew we could always find a safe, secure, high-paying job. Both of us were college graduates with good job skills and a solid work ethic. But we weren't going for job security. We were going for financial freedom.

By 1989, we were millionaires.

I often hear people say, "It takes money to make money." That's B.S.—and I don't mean a Bachelor of Science degree! Our journey from homelessness to being millionaires in four years, and then on to genuine financial freedom in another five years, did *not* take money. We *had* no money when we started—in fact, we were in debt—and nobody gave us anything along the way, either.

It also does not take a good formal education. A college education is important for traditional professions, but not for people looking to build wealth.

If it doesn't take money to make money, and it doesn't take a formal education to learn how to become financially free, then what does it take? It takes a dream, a

CHAPTER 6: It's Time to Take Control!

lot of determination, a willingness to learn quickly, and an understanding of which sector of the cashflow quadrant you're operating in.

Hard Work Will Not Make You Rich

There is this strange idea in our culture that says, "If you work really hard, you'll be okay." What a pile of baloney! And what's so tragic about it is that most people have been brainwashed to believe it, and they *do* believe it, even though we're all surrounded by tons of evidence to the contrary.

What evidence? Just look around you. Do you know anyone who has worked really hard his entire life, only to end up living a life that hovers just above—or just below—the indignity and heartbreak called "subsistence level"?

Of course you do. We all do. The world is full of people who work hard and are most definitely *not* okay. And perhaps the worst part about it is that many of these unfortunates come to the conclusion that it was their fault, their personal failing. They did all the right things, right? But it still didn't work. Maybe they just didn't try hard enough, or didn't get the lucky breaks. Maybe they were just not cut out for success.

Nonsense. The problem is that the hard-work myth is just that: a myth.

Now, don't get me wrong. I'm not saying that building wealth and financial freedom doesn't take hard work; it does, and lots of it. I hope you're not naïve enough to believe the idiots who will tell you they can show a way to wealth that's easy, that's quick, or that's painless. Because if you are, I know a bridge you can buy real cheap—and an entire system of subprime mortgages and credit-default swaps that might be just right for you.

No, it takes hard work, all right. The question is, hard work doing what?

I can already hear you thinking, "Doing what?! Making money, of course!" But not so fast, because here's the cold, hard truth lurking behind that sad error of our culture's thinking:

Working hard at making money will never create wealth.

People who work for income work harder and harder, only to be taxed more and more. Forget working hard at making money: All you'll do is spend it, and then have to work hard all over again.

You might be asking, "Okay, so what do I do?" You *take* control.

Take control of what? After all, most things in life you *cannot* control, no matter how hard you try. You can't control the market. You can't control employees. You can't control the economy. What *can* you control? You can control the source of your income.

The Problem

Building a business is the way most of the very rich became rich. Bill Gates built Microsoft; Michael Dell created Dell Computers in his dormitory room. Still, historically, there have been very, very few people who have truly lived in the B quadrant. The B quadrant is the best place to begin generating genuine wealth, but at the same, there are some barriers to entry that have kept most people out.

For one thing, most people don't have the cash it takes to start their own business. Today it costs an average of $5 million to start your own business. And for another thing, building your own business from scratch remains the riskiest of all ways to become rich. The failure rate for new businesses is about 90 percent in the first five years—and if your new venture fails, guess who just lost $5 million? In my early years of starting businesses, I failed twice, and while it never pushed me into bankruptcy (and I never got any government bailouts!), it did cost me millions of dollars.

Typically when you start your own business, you have to make sure your rent, utilities, and the rest of your overhead are paid, your employees are paid, and your suppliers are paid, or you're out of business. So guess who doesn't get paid? You. In the course of starting a new business—and I'm talking here about a *successful* business—you can easily go five to ten years without taking a paycheck.

Remember Kim and me, sleeping in our beat-up Toyota? It wasn't fun. We could have taken jobs that would have immediately put a roof over our heads, but as miserable as it was (and believe me, it was), we chose homelessness over employment because we believed in our dream of being business owners and living in the B quadrant.

Most people do not have the mental, emotional, physical, or financial stamina to handle these conditions. It can be brutal, and usually is.

What About a Franchise?

A franchise takes a great part of the risk out of it. With an established franchise like McDonald's or Subway, your odds of success improve significantly, and a lot of the groundwork is done for you. But you're still stuck with problem No. 1: You have to come up with the cash. The cost of purchasing one of the better-known franchises can range from $100,000 to $1.5 million or even more, and that's just for the rights to the franchise. Then there are monthly payments to headquarters for training, advertising, and support.

And even all this support is still no guarantee of great wealth. Many times a person must continue to pay money to the franchisor or headquarters, even when his or her personal franchise is losing money. Even if you are one of those who succeeds at a franchise, chances are very good that you still won't make any money yourself for the first few years. And one in three franchises eventually go broke.

When my poor dad was 50 years old, he had the temerity to run for governor of Hawaii—and the incumbent he was running against happened to be his boss. Not only did he lose the election, but his boss fired him and told him he'd never work in

Hawaii again. He took all his savings and used it to buy a popular franchise, one that was billed as a "never-lose franchise."

The franchise that couldn't lose lost, and so did my dad. In fact, he lost everything.

In theory, a franchise is a great idea, but in reality, it's a gamble—and it's a gamble where you have to pony up a fortune just to sidle up to the table and play.

The Power of Passive Income

Have you ever used one of those spring-loaded water faucets that some public restrooms install to save water? When you turn the water on, you have to hold the faucet there, because when you let go, it bounces back to the off position.

Most people's income source works just like that faucet: You get a little money flowing, and then when you let go, it bounces back to off. You can never build freedom that way. What you want is a money faucet that you can let go of once you've turned it on, *because it stays on by itself.*

It's not just about having income today, tomorrow, and next week; it's about securing your income in perpetuity. This is *passive income*, also known as *residual income*: income that continues coming in, over and over, long after you finished expending the effort and capital it took to create the source of the income.

Shifting yourself into the B quadrant is a strong step in that direction, but not all businesses will create passive income. If you own a restaurant, you earn income only when you prepare and sell a meal. If your business fixes air conditioners, you earn income only when you provide that service. Even high-salaried doctors and lawyers earn money only when they see patients or clients. If no patients or clients require their knowledge and services in a particular week, the income faucet springs shut again and there's no money coming in that week.

What most people need is an avenue to create passive income. Knowing this, Donald Trump and I teamed up to evaluate the many kinds of business structures that can create passive income, and published our results in a book, *We Want You to Be Rich*.

And by the way, that's not just a book title. We do want you to be rich. Wealth is not a zero-sum game; it's not like if you become rich, then you're taking it away from me, or Donald, or anyone else. This is an astonishing and abundant world we live in, and there is way more than enough energy, material, ingenuity, creativity, and ambition to allow *every human being* on the planet to be wealthy.

So what did we discover? We found that one business model stood out from the rest. This particular business model creates passive income, but requires relatively little cash investment to start up. It has very low overhead, and can be operated on a flexible part-time basis until it generates enough cash flow for the entrepreneur to transition out of his current full-time job.

That business model is called *network marketing*, and it's what the rest of this book is all about.

PART TWO

One Business—Eight Wealth-Building Assets
*Eight reasons network marketing
can secure your future*

CHAPTER 7

My Years in the Business

I need to start here with full disclosure: I've never *really* been "in" the business of network marketing. I am not a distributor for or owner of a network marketing company, have no financial interests in any network marketing company, and do not promote any one specific company. But I have been very much *in* the business for years as a champion and advocate of the network marketing business as a whole, and in this chapter I want to tell you why.

I first encountered network marketing in 1975, when a friend invited me to a presentation on a new business opportunity. Since I make it a habit to investigate business and investment opportunities, I agreed to go, although I thought it was a little strange that the business meeting was at a private home rather than in an office.

I listened for three hours while he talked about the value of building your own business instead of working at a job. I agreed with most of the points he made. At the end of the evening, the friend asked me what I thought about what I'd heard. "It's interesting," I replied, "but it's not for me."

I was already thoroughly involved in the process of building a business. Why would I need to build a business with other people? And besides, *it was network marketing*. I really had no idea what that meant, but I *thought* I knew what it meant, and I was sure it held no value for me.

Soon after my first network marketing meeting, the sports wallet business that I had started with two friends boomed. My two years of hard work started paying off. Success, fame, and fortune seemed to pour down upon my two partners and me. We had pledged we would all be millionaires by the age of 30, and through our hard work and sacrifice, we had reached our goal. (And this was the 1970s, when a million dollars was actually worth something.) Our company and products were written up in such magazines as *Surfer*, *Runner's World*, and *Gentleman's Quarterly*. We were the hot new thing in the sporting goods world, and business poured in from all over the globe. I was an all-out success.

I never gave network marketing another thought—at least, not for the next decade.

CHAPTER 7: My Years in the Business

The Opening of a Mind

Over the years that followed, my mind began to open up. That incredibly successful business failed a few years after it started. It was a humbling experience, and a very positive one, because it caused me to look closer at the world around me and to ask questions. More of what my rich dad had taught me began to sink in, and my perspective grew. It was not long before I had built another successful business, and then another, and then another—and unlike that first business, these lasted.

I came to realize that while personal success is fulfilling, it's much more fulfilling when you can help many others create their own success as well.

During those years, I also became powerfully drawn to the idea of not only becoming rich myself, but also finding ways to help others become rich. I came to realize that while personal success is fulfilling, it's much more fulfilling when you can help many others create their own success as well.

For the next fifteen years, I kept hearing negative things about network marketing, mostly from people I knew. Eventually, I decided to check it out for myself.

In the early 1990s, I ran into a friend named Bill who was a retired multimillionaire. We got talking, and lo and behold, Bill told me that he was involved in building a network marketing business!

Bill is a very sharp, very savvy guy. I knew he had just completed commercial real estate projects worth over $1 billion. I asked him why on earth he was involved in network marketing.

"For years," he told me, "people have asked me for real estate investment tips. They want to know if they can invest with me. But they can't, because most don't have the $50,000 or $100,000 it takes to get into my level of real estate investments.

"In fact, many of them have absolutely no money at all. Some are two paychecks away from bankruptcy. So they look for these cheap, no-money-down deals that are often very bad investments. In network marketing, I can actually help people make the kind of money they need to do some serious investing. The more people I help do that, the more investors I have!

"Besides," he added, "I really love working with people who are hungry to learn and grow. It's a drag working with people who think they already know it all, which is what often ends up happening in my real estate deals. The people I work with in network marketing are genuinely excited about new ideas."

After a few more minutes of conversation, I had to make a dash for the airport, but over the next few months, we continued our dialogue, and as we did, my respect for network marketing and what it represented grew.

In 1994, I started researching the industry in earnest. I went to every presentation I heard about and listened closely to everything I heard. I studied the literature of company after company, looked at their track records, and examined them closely, the way I would do my due diligence on any business venture I was considering investing in. I even joined a few companies, if I liked what I saw, just so I could learn more about them and see what the experience was like from the inside.

Eventually, I began meeting some of these companies' leaders, and I was stunned to find that they were some of the most intelligent, kind, ethical, moral, spiritual, and professional people I had met in all my years of business. Once I got over my own prejudices and met people I respected and related to, I saw that I had found the heart of the industry—and I was amazed at what I had found.

When I had first stumbled upon the concept in that first opportunity meeting in 1975, my mind had been closed tight to the idea. Now, some twenty years later, my view had completely changed.

People sometimes ask me, "Why do you recommend network marketing to people as a way they can build wealth, when you did not become rich that way yourself?"

Actually, it is *because* I did not gain my fortune through network marketing that I can be a bit more objective about the industry. I came to appreciate this business as an outsider, and only after I had already built my own wealth and established my own financial freedom.

All the same, if I had to do it all over again today and start from scratch, rather than building an old-style business, I would start out by building a network marketing business.

So What Exactly Is Network Marketing?

I said that I've never actually been involved in network marketing as a participant, but I know someone who has, and I invited him to join me in these pages to share some of his insights.

My friend John Fleming started out in life as an architect (he once worked for the legendary Mies van der Rohe), and that's one of the reasons I admire his approach to network marketing: He brings that same passion for practical design and functional construction to this business. He's a man, in other words, who appreciates the value of building structures that last.

John brings to these pages his nearly forty years of experience in network marketing. He has owned and operated his own company and has held many different executive positions in others, including a fifteen-year tenure at one of the industry's largest and most well-respected companies as a regional vice president and then vice president of sales strategy, training, and development. He has also been actively involved in the industry's various trade groups; in 1997 the Direct Selling Education Foundation awarded John with its highest honor, their Circle of Honor Award. Today, John serves as publisher and editor in chief of *Direct Selling News*, a respected trade publication serving direct selling and network marketing executives.

CHAPTER 7: My Years in the Business

Robert: John, for those readers who may not already know, what exactly is network marketing, and what makes it tick?

John: Network marketing has been around in various forms since the middle of the last century. The basic idea is as simple as it is brilliant: Instead of spending tons of money on all sorts of professional agencies and marketing channels to promote products or services, why not pay the people who love them most to just tell others about them?

That's exactly what a network marketing company does: They pay a portion of every sales dollar received back out to their field of independent representatives, who typically are also the products' most committed and enthusiastic consumers.

Robert: Let me play devil's advocate for a moment. How can that really work? I mean, can a bunch of ordinary people who are not skilled marketers really compete and generate any serious level of sales?

John: Actually, that's the beauty of it. As every marketing professional, Hollywood producer, and corporate giant knows, the single most powerful form of promotion in the world is personal word-of-mouth. That's why television commercials spend millions to hire actors to talk just like your mom, your spouse, your best friend, or your kids: They are imitating personal word-of-mouth.

In network marketing, we use the real thing. The real power of the model—what you talk about, Robert, as *leverage*—is that as a representative, you aren't paid commissions only on products used by the people you refer to the company, but often on products bought by the people *they* refer, directly and indirectly, that can really add up.

So, does it work? You know the answer to that one: Direct selling/network marketing today does well over $110 billion in annual sales globally, which makes it an economic bloc roughly the size of New Zealand, Pakistan, or the Philippines. (I often describe this business model with both the terms "direct selling" and "network marketing" because today, most direct selling companies employ a network marketing focus. However, for the purposes of this book, I will just use "network marketing" in my references.)

One reason that the total sales from network marketing keeps growing is that it's a true win-win. The company gets an amazing level of market penetration and customer awareness that would be very tough and very expensive to get with traditional marketing. And the independent rep has the opportunity to create significant cash flow.

How? By harnessing the power of word-of-mouth—person-to-person relationships—to build a substantial network that represents the company's line of products and/or services.

Robert, you talk about a B quadrant business being one that has at least 500 employees. In network marketing, you don't hire employees, you sponsor individuals who are all independent representatives. But the same financial dynamic applies: By the time your network of independent representatives grows to be 300, 400, or 500 strong, you've got a serious organization that delivers significant residual income.

What Others Say About Network Marketing

As John says, the model is powerful because *it works*—and we're not the only ones who say so, either.

Tom Peters, the legendary management expert and author of the classic best-seller *In Search of Excellence*, describes network marketing as "the first truly revolutionary shift in marketing since the advent of 'modern' marketing at Procter and Gamble and Harvard Business School over fifty years ago."

The emerging success of network marketing has been written about in such journals as *Forbes, Fortune, Newsweek, TIME, U.S. News & World Report, USA Today, The New York Times,* and *The Wall Street Journal*. Fifteen years ago, you couldn't have gotten a single one of these journals to give this business the time of day. Now, look at what a recent issue of *Fortune* said about network marketing:

Today, network marketing is recognized by many experts and accomplished businesspeople as one of the fastest-growing business models in the world.

"An investor's dream ... the best-kept secret of the business world ... an industry with steady annual growth, healthy cash flows, high return on invested capital, and long-term prospects for global expansion."

Warren Buffett and Richard Branson couldn't be more different. Buffett drives a pickup and lives in Omaha; Branson flies his own airline and lives on his own island in the British Virgin Islands. But they have three things in common. They are both billionaires. They are both extremely practical men. And they have both owned network marketing companies.

Does that tell you something?

Citigroup, Jockey, L'Oréal, Mars, Remington, and Unilever: Guess what they all have in common? They've all put a toe in the network marketing water—in some cases, right up to their hips.

Today, network marketing is recognized by many experts and accomplished businesspeople as one of the fastest-growing business models in the world.

CHAPTER 8

It's Not About Income—
It's About Assets That Generate Income

It's no wonder so many people don't understand the value of network marketing: Many of those who are actually involved with it themselves don't fully grasp the value of what they hold in their hands.

When people go to hear network marketing presentations, often their main question is, "If I join this business, how much income can I earn here?" And no surprise, when you listen to people promote their network marketing business, often that's exactly what you will hear them talk about: how much you can earn on a per-month basis.

The reason people want to know how much they can earn per month is that they are thinking in terms of living in the E quadrant or S quadrant. They are thinking about supplementing or replacing their current E quadrant or S quadrant income.

But that's not where the real value of network marketing lies.

The problem with earning income is that it's an incredibly limited, linear process. Work an hour, earn a dollar; work two hours, earn two dollars. It depends on you, which means you can never stop. As I said before, it's a trap. Most people instinctively sense that, but they assume that the way out of the trap is to earn more income. But earning more income doesn't change the basic fact of being tied to your income. In fact, often earning more income only serves to draw the noose tighter.

The B and I quadrants are not about earning more income; they're about owning assets that *generate* income.

The Truth About Your House

The things that most people think of as assets are not assets at all; in fact, they're liabilities.

What defines whether something is an asset or a liability is cash flow, not some abstraction of value. In other words, is it generating money that goes into your pocket, or is it taking money out of your pocket? Everything will either make you money or cost you money. If it doesn't make you money, it's not an asset, it's a liability.

For years now, people have been using their houses as ATMs, borrowing against them to scarf up cash they could use to pay off their credit cards, take vacations, buy that SUV, whatever. Maybe you've done this yourself. If you have, the reason you did is that you bought the conventional line that your house was an asset, and not what it really is: a credit card with shingles and a driveway.

Let me explain what an asset is.

Most people are so confused about this that they have it backward. They run to the dictionary and find that an asset is something that's "worth something." Well, maybe. The problem is that tricky word, *worth*. Let me ask you a question:

What is your house worth?

Before you answer, let me ask you the same question a different way:

How much income does your house bring you, month in and month out?

Chances are good your answer is, "Well, none—in fact, I spend a good chunk of change on it every month, in upkeep, repair, and so forth."

Exactly. That's because *your house is not an asset; it's a liability.*

"But wait a minute," you say, "my house is worth a couple hundred thousand!"

Oh, really? When? When you sell it, at some theoretical point in the future? But then where would you live? Would you take the proceeds of your sale and buy another house to live in? Of course. So where's the worth, the actual discretionary income that you can hold in your hands and use to buy or invest in anything you like? It isn't there: There isn't any. *Your house is not an asset; it's a hole in the ground into which you pour money.*

How to Know Your Asset from a Hole in the Ground

Forget the dictionary definition for a moment. Let's talk about the real world. An asset is something that works for you, so you don't have to work for the rest of your life. My poor dad always said, "Work for a job." My rich dad said, "Build assets."

The powerful thing about living in the B quadrant is that when you build a business, you are building an asset.

In our Rich Dad business, we have offices throughout the world. Whether I'm working or sleeping or playing golf, the checks come in. That's passive income: residual income. While I won't work hard for a job, I'll work really hard to build an asset, simply because I think like a rich person, not like a working-class person.

Because owning a business is owning an asset, when you build a network marketing business, you're not only learning critical life skills, you're also building a genuine asset for yourself. In a job, you earn income. In network marketing, instead of earning income, you build an asset—your business—and t*he asset generates income.*

I only invest in things that make me money. If it makes me money, it's an asset; if it takes money from me, it's a liability. I have two Porsches. They're liabilities. I own them free and clear, but they're not putting money in my pocket; they're taking money out of my pocket. It's not rocket science.

For people who understand this, the No. 1 asset is usually a business, and the No. 2 asset is typically real estate. And even with real estate, you have to understand the difference between cash flow and capital gain. Most people don't understand this distinction. When they invest, they invest for capital gain. They'll say, "My house went up in value. My car went up in value." That's capital gain, not cash flow.

The purpose of owning real estate is to keep it as an asset, not to sell it for a profit. If you buy a piece of real estate for $100,000 and then sell it for $200,000, that's not an asset; you just generated a $100,000 capital gain. You had to shoot the asset to get that money. You've killed the asset. It's like selling your cow for money. I'd rather own the cow and sell the milk.

This is the biggest problem with having a job: A job is not an asset. You can't sell it on eBay; you can't rent it out; you can't take dividends from it. Why spend decades, the best years of your life, working away to build something that is not an asset? Or, to put it more accurately, to build *someone else's* asset, but not your own?

Because make no mistake about it: When you work at a job, you are building an asset—it's just not *your* asset.

We've had this idea drilled into us that there is some sort of inherent value in having a good job, but there is absolutely no value in it—zero. And to add insult to injury, the income from your job is then taxed at a higher rate than any other form of income. Talk about the deck being stacked against you! Yet that is the price some people are willing to pay for the "safety and security" of the E quadrant.

Network Marketing Is Not About Selling Products or Earning Income!

The biggest popular misconception about network marketing is that it's a *selling* business. But selling is just earning more income. The problem is, if you stop the activity, the income stops.

A salesperson has a job. If you work behind the counter at a department store, you're in the E quadrant; if you're in business for yourself, selling insurance or homes or jewelry, you're in the S quadrant. But either way, you have a job, and your job is to sell.

That's not going to build your wealth or your freedom.

What you want is not another job; you want *another address*, one over in the B quadrant.

John: Robert, that's exactly right. People often assume that being successful in this business means being "great at sales." But the point of network marketing is not to become great at selling your particular product or service, because no matter how good you might be at doing that—and let's be honest, if you're like most people, you don't think you *are* very good at it—there's only so much income you can earn selling.

After all, there are so many hours in the day, right?

In network marketing, the whole point is not to *sell a product* but to *build a network*, an army of people who are all representing that same product or service to share with others.

The goal is not for you or any other individual to sell a lot of product; it's for *a lot of people* to be their own best customer, sell and service a reasonable number of customers, and recruit and show a lot of other people how to do the same thing.

And here's the reason you want to build that army of independent representatives: Once you do, you know what you'll have? An asset that generates income for you—*passive* income.

In Chapter 13, I'll ask John to explain more fully why network marketing is not about selling or being a salesperson, and I hope you pay really close attention, because this is a key point—one that most people just don't get. For now, here's the key nail I want to hammer home: *Network marketing is not about earning more income; it's about building an asset.*

Actually, it's about building *eight* assets, all at the same time. And in the next chapters, we'll take a look at each one in turn.

CHAPTER 9

Asset #1: *A Real-World Business Education*

I have a confession to make: I am a slow reader. I do read a lot, it's just that I read very slowly, and I often have to read a book two or three times before I really understand what I'm reading. What's more, I am also a very poor writer; in fact, I failed writing twice in high school.

So you want to know something ironic? This C student, who failed his writing courses in school and who to this day is not a very good writer, has had seven books on *The New York Times* best-seller list.

My point? Good grades aren't everything.

Don't get me wrong: I'm not putting down education. I believe in education; in fact, I believe in it with a passion. It's just that the education I believe in most is the education that truly teaches you what you need to learn to be successful in your life.

When I recommend that people build their own network marketing business, the No. 1 reason I always give is not for the many excellent, even life-changing products you might represent. And it's not for the money you can earn or the financial freedom you can create.

Yes, the products are often excellent. And, yes, I put a great deal of value on its ability to give you a real path to building wealth. But these are not *the* most important benefits you gain from the experience. The No. 1 value you get from the experience is a *real-world business education*.

Three Kinds of Education

If you want to be financially successful, there are three different types of education you require: scholastic, professional, and financial education.

Scholastic education teaches you how to read, write, and do math. It is a very important education, especially in today's world. Personally, I did not do well with this level of education. As I've said, I was a C student most of my life, simply because I was not that interested in what I was being taught.

CHAPTER 9: *Asset #1:* A Real-World Business Education

Professional education teaches you how to work for money. In other words, it prepares you for life in the E and S quadrants. During my youth, the smart kids went on to become doctors, lawyers, and accountants. Others went to professional schools that taught them to become medical assistants, plumbers, builders, electricians, and automobile mechanics.

I didn't excel here, either. Since I had not done well at scholastic education, I was not encouraged to become a doctor, lawyer, or accountant. Instead, I became a ship's officer and then a helicopter pilot, flying for the Marine Corps in Vietnam. By the time I was 23 years old, I had two professions, one as a ship's officer and the other as a pilot, but I never really used either of them to make money.

Financial education is where you learn to have *money work for you* rather than to have *you work for money*. You might think you'd get a financial education in business school, but by and large, that's not what happens. What business schools generally do is take the smartest kids and train them to be business executives for the rich. In other words, they train their students for life in the upper echelon of the E quadrant—but it's *still* the E quadrant.

After I returned from Vietnam, I considered going back to school to get my MBA, but my rich dad talked me out of it. He said, "If you get an MBA from a traditional school, you are being trained to be an employee of the rich. If you want to be rich yourself, you don't need more scholastic education, you need a real-world financial education."

The Important Skills

Being an entrepreneur and building a B quadrant business is not easy. In fact, I believe building a B quadrant business is one of the toughest challenges a person can take on. The reason there are so many more people in the E and S quadrants is that those quadrants are less demanding than the B quadrant. If it were easy, everyone would be doing it.

If you are going to be successful in business, there are technical skills you need to learn that you probably did not learn in school.

For example, the ability to get organized and set your own agenda.

This is bigger than it might sound. People who enter the arena of network marketing sometimes experience a type of culture shock, because they are used to being told what to do. You may work very, very hard in the E quadrant, yet have absolutely no experience at setting goals, organizing a plan of action, setting your agenda, managing your time, and executing a clear sequence of productive actions.

It's shocking how many people do not have these basic skills. Shocking, but not surprising. After all, in the E quadrant, you really don't need them. But if you're entering the B quadrant, they are not an option. They are every bit as important as skills like knowing how to balance a checkbook, write a financial plan, and read an annual report.

Tax Advantages—and the Lesson They Teach

People who are brand-new to network marketing are often quite surprised to learn about the significant tax advantages that come from having your own home-based business.

Most people have at least a vague idea that the rich enjoy all sorts of tax advantages that they themselves do not, but since they have lived their entire lives within the E quadrant, they typically have no concept of what those advantages are or how they actually work. Therefore, people are often shocked to realize that they, too, can enjoy those very same tax advantages and put significant amounts of money in their pockets from the very first day of their new businesses.

With recent changes in tax policies and more insurance programs tailored for small businesses and the self-employed, it's easier than ever before to create your own benefits package that rivals and even surpasses anything the standard big corporation could offer. By starting a network marketing business in your spare time and keeping your regular job, you begin to gain the tax advantages of the rich. A person with a part-time business can take more tax deductions than employees can.

| home office | auto, gas, mileage | home computer | internet & telecom | travel, dining, hotel | personal product use |

The above are just some examples of things you already spend money on that may become legitimate tax deductions once you begin your own home-based network marketing business. Note: This list is given here for illustration purposes only; for tax advice on your own situation, you should consult your tax professional.

For example, you may be able to deduct car expenses, gasoline, some meals, and entertainment. Obviously, you need to check with a CPA for exact rulings on your situation. And when you do, you'll find that *the cost of that visit to your CPA is tax-deductible, too!* In other words, the government will actually give you a tax break for the cost of getting professional advice on how to pay the government less in taxes.

One of the beauties of network marketing is that it pulls away the veil of mystery and starts to show you life in the B quadrant.

My point in going into all this is not only to let you know about this significant economic leverage that comes on Day One of your new business from tax savings.

CHAPTER 9: *Asset #1:* A Real-World Business Education

More than that, I wanted to drive home this point: Most people have no clue what it's like to be in the B quadrant!

The reason most people are shocked when they learn about the tax advantages available here is that, for the great majority of people, the B quadrant might as well be the lost continent of Atlantis. One of the beauties of network marketing is that it pulls away the veil of mystery and starts to show you life in the B quadrant.

Welcome to your real-world business education.

Life Skills

When it comes to creating business success, it's not a simple matter of technical skills. Even more important are the life skills it takes to successfully negotiate the B quadrant. The key to long-term success in life is your education and skills, your life experiences, and most of all, your personal character.

For example, I had to learn how to overcome my self-doubt, shyness, and fear of rejection. Another personal-development skill I had to learn was how to pick myself up after I failed and keep going. These are the personal traits a person must develop if they are to be successful in a B quadrant business, regardless whether it is a network marketing business, a franchise, or an entrepreneurial startup.

If you don't learn these things in school, and you don't learn them in the workplace, and you were not taught them in your home while growing up, where are you going to learn them? Where on earth will you find a business that will invest the time in your education and personal development as well as help you actually build your business?

In network marketing, that's where.

John: It's interesting, Robert, that you always cite the business education as the No. 1 benefit you see in the business, and I think there's a lot of merit to that point. Often, people learn skills and develop aspects of themselves through their experience in network marketing that they might otherwise never learn.

Network marketing teaches people how to overcome their fears, how to communicate, how to understand the psychology of other people saying "No" to them, and how to maintain persistence in the face of rejection and other real-world challenges.

Here are some of the critical skills that the real-world education of network marketing teaches:

- An attitude of success
- Dressing for success
- Overcoming personal fears, doubts, and lack of confidence
- Overcoming the fear of rejection
- Communication skills
- People skills
- Time-management skills

- Accountability skills
- Practical goal-setting
- Money-management skills
- Investing skills

Good network marketing companies provide a solid program of training in all these areas. And I agree: This kind of education is absolutely priceless.

In fact, you'd be hard-pressed to find a situation anywhere else where you could pay good money to gain all this training—let alone a situation where *they pay you* to learn it.

We have a common expression in network marketing, that it's a business "where you earn while you learn." It's a great saying, because it underlines this key point about the business: You learn to do it *by doing it*, not by sitting in a classroom for years hearing someone talk about doing it.

Network marketing is a real-world business school for people who want to learn the real-world skills of an entrepreneur, rather than the skills of an employee.

In network marketing, the training is more than theory; it's experiential. And regardless of whether or not you reach the top of the specific program you're in or make a great deal of money, the training itself is of tremendous value for the rest of your life. Many people actually end up in other businesses where they become very successful due to the business training and experience they first received in their network marketing experience.

And that's the real point here, and the biggest reason that I've been recommending this business to people for a decade. When you join a good network marketing company, they don't just give you a track to run on, they also support you in developing the skills and qualities you need to succeed.

Network marketing is a real-world business school for people who want to learn the real-world skills of an entrepreneur, rather than the skills of an employee.

CHAPTER 10

Asset #2: *A Profitable Path of Personal Development*

I know what you're probably saying. "Kiyosaki, have you gone soft?! What's all this touchy-feely talk about a 'path of personal development'? I don't need an encounter group; I need to make ends meet. I want to build wealth, not sing 'Kumbaya'!"

Not so fast. I haven't gone soft on you: I'm just being realistic. Becoming rich is not about putting your lucky fifty-cent piece into the right slot machine. And you are not simply looking at a new way to earn a supplemental income. You are actually making a change in your core values. It's not just about changing what you do; in a very real sense, it's about changing who you *are*.

My friend Donald Trump is worth billions today, but there was a time when he lost it all during a real estate crash. He talks about the experience of being $9.2 billion in debt: "I passed a beggar on the street and realized he was worth $9.2 billion more than I was!" Yet, before long, Donald was back on top again. Why? Because of who he *is*—or more accurately, who he had become.

I had a similar experience. By age 30, I was a millionaire. Two years later, my company had gone broke. Losing a business was not a pleasant experience, but it was a great education. I learned a lot in those few years—a lot about business, but even more about myself.

After the crash, rich dad told me, "Money and success make you arrogant and stupid. Now, with some poverty and humility behind you, you can become a student again." He was right. The lessons I learned from the experience proved over time to be priceless. Building and then losing a worldwide business provided me with a real-world education that ultimately made me rich. Even more important, it was an education that set me free. And the most important things I learned in the course of that education were not about business or money—they were about *me*.

Let me ask John a question about this, and if his answer is what I think it's going to be, you'll see what I mean.

CHAPTER 10: *Asset #2:* A Profitable Path of Personal Development

Robert: John, obviously not everyone who goes into network marketing has the same level of success. In your experience, what is the No. 1 reason that some people fail to reach the level of success they hoped for in network marketing?

John: Success is defined differently by different people. What may be important for one person may not be for another. Some people are satisfied with supplementing their current level of income, while others are truly looking for a business opportunity that can be transforming, in terms of income potential and lifestyle goals. You have to define failure in a very broad sense. Being able to earn $1,000 a month may be seen as failure for the person who was attempting to build a significant business, but great success for the mother whose goal was to significantly supplement the household income.

Regardless of the goal, we know that those who persist in network marketing tend to get only better and better. In fact, the only way I believe people fail is to quit.

But this needs a little but more detail to be fully accurate. It's not simply a matter of whether or not one quits the company—that is, resigns one's distributorship and formally declares, "I'm out." The issue here is not about quitting the business; it's about *quitting on yourself.*

That's exactly what I thought. It goes back to what I said at the very beginning of this book: This isn't just about changing the type of business you're working with; it's also about changing *you.* I can show you the perfect business, but for your business to grow, you will have to grow as well.

The Winner in You—and the Loser in You

There are two words for what John just described. One is *quitter;* the other is *loser.*

Each of us has a winner and a loser inside of us. That includes me, too: There's a winner in me and a loser in me, and they often compete for air time. The reason most people "just get by" instead of truly succeeding in life is that they let the loser inside them dominate. I don't. I insist that the winner win out.

How do you know when the loser is speaking up? "Oh, I can't afford that." "Oh, that's too risky." Or, "What if I fail?" The winner is up for the risk, but the loser thinks only of safety and security.

It's ironic. The loser yaps and squawks about safety and security—and ends up stuck in a career and a life that is never truly safe or secure. What's safe about working a forty-hour-a-week job for a corporation that will probably lay you off within the next few years? Or sticking your meager earnings into a 401(k) that gets sucked up by a mutual fund that tanks, or into a fund managed by a financial advisor who turns out to be another Bernie Madoff?

Inside each of us is the winner and the loser, the rich guy and the poor guy, the one who works out and the one who sits on the couch. That's the battle. The reason you want to join a network marketing company is that they will support the rich person inside of you to stand up and be counted. Your loser friends want you to stay on the couch, they want you to play it safe and work your forty hours, because if you do, then you won't be challenging them to do anything different. Not your network marketing sponsor. Your network marketing team wants to see you excel, to step beyond what you're used to doing, to go beyond your history and become the more exceptional, extraordinary you, instead of remaining the ordinary you.

It's easy to say, "I can't afford that," or, "It's just too expensive," or, "I just want my benefits; I don't want to have to work that hard or take those risks." That's the loser speaking.

And you shouldn't feel bad about that. We've all got one. I have one in me, and lots of times he gets the upper hand—at least for a short time. Every morning, I make that choice: Who got up this morning, the rich me or the poor me? The winner or the loser? That's our battle.

In fact, we each have an entire cast of characters inside us, a whole spectrum of who we could potentially turn out to be. I wanted the person who was happily married, who made a contribution to the planet, and who was spiritually inclined for freedom.

Every time we let our fears, our doubts, or our low self-esteem win, the loser emerges and holds sway. Learning to share your vision and tell a powerful, persuasive story is learning how to override the loser inside you and allowing the winner to rise to the surface. Learning how to tell a powerful story is learning how to show up as the winner you are.

Most people don't have the ability to keep going, to handle disappointment and never lose sight of the vision of where they're going. They simply haven't been trained in that skill. But that's critically important. That's the real skill of someone who has mastered the B quadrant. That is thinking like an entrepreneur—and that's the single most important attribute you can learn from building your own network marketing business.

It took me two full years, when I first went to work for Xerox Corporation, to begin stepping into my power and letting the winner in me emerge. I was on the brink of being fired at the end of those two years, but fortunately for me, that's when my self-confidence finally began to grow. My sales improved, and within another two years, I was consistently No. 1 or No. 2 in my office.

Network marketing gives you the opportunity to face your fears, deal with them, overcome them, and bring out the winner that you have living inside you.

Increasing my self-esteem was more important than my paycheck. Rebuilding my self-confidence and my self-esteem has been priceless. And it has helped me earn millions of dollars. For that, I will always be grateful to the Xerox Corporation and the staff that taught me how to overcome my demons, doubts, and fears. Today, I strongly recommend network marketing because the industry offers the same opportunity to strengthen and rebuild your self-confidence that the Xerox Corporation offered me.

Network marketing gives you the opportunity to face your fears, deal with them, overcome them, and bring out the winner that you have living inside you.

And make no mistake about it—just because you join a network marketing company and start building your business doesn't mean you have left the loser behind. It will take years to build up your genuine freedom. We talk a lot about freedom in this country. But you don't really *have* freedom until you have *financial* freedom. And that takes time to create.

I was born with nothing, and I made and lost my fortune several times along the way, so I know what it feels like to lose everything: It's easy, in those difficult times, for the loser to take over. There will be times when you will feel tested; when your friends are telling you, "I told you so," and your family members are whispering to you, "Don't you think it'd be better if you just put more energy into your little job and let that network thing go?"

I promise you, there will be times when it will be so tempting to let the loser run the show. Don't do it.

Win!

Flight School

All caterpillars make cocoons before becoming butterflies. Flight school was my cocoon. I entered as a college graduate and exited a pilot ready to go to Vietnam.

If I had gone to a civilian flight school, I doubt I would have been ready for war, even though I was a pilot. What we had to learn as military pilots is far different from what civilian pilots have to learn. The skills are different, the intensity of training is different, and the reality of going to war at the end of the training makes things different.

It took me nearly two years to get through basic flight school in Florida. I received my wings, and then was transferred to advanced flight training at Camp Pendleton, California. The training there escalated in its intensity: At Camp Pendleton, we were trained to fight more than to fly.

After we had finished flight school and became pilots, we had one year to prepare to go to Vietnam. We flew constantly, often under conditions that tested us mentally, emotionally, physically, and spiritually.

About eight months into the program at Camp Pendleton, something changed inside me. During one training flight, I finally became a pilot who was ready to go to war. Up to that point, I was flying mentally, emotionally, and physically. Some people call it "flying mechanically." On that one training mission, I changed spiritually. The mission was so intense and frightening that, suddenly, all my doubts and fears were forced out of the way, and my human spirit took over. Flying had become a part of me. I felt at peace and at home inside the aircraft. The aircraft was part of me. I was ready to go to Vietnam.

It was not that I had no fear. I still had the same fears about going to war—the fear of dying or, even worse, of becoming crippled. The difference was that I was now ready to go to war. My confidence in myself was greater than the fears.

My process of becoming a businessperson and investor followed much the same process as becoming a pilot ready to go into battle. It took my failing twice in business before I suddenly found that quality that is often called *entrepreneurial spirit*. That is the spirit that keeps me on the B and I side of the cashflow quadrant map, no matter how tough things get. I stay on the B and I side rather than slipping back to the safety and comfort of the E and S side.

I would say it took me fifteen years to gain the confidence to feel comfortable in the B quadrant. You're luckier than I am: You don't need to spend that long or go through the failures and struggles I did. You can get that same kind of life-changing education right here in your own flight school: network marketing.

How My Business Skills Changed My Life

Now that I've talked about military training and learning to fly under battle conditions in the jungles of Vietnam, I want to tell you one more story about the honing of character—this one not on the battlefield, but in the field of love.

If I had not gone through my own intense form of schooling to learn real-world business skills, I doubt I would have been fortunate enough to marry the woman of my dreams. But I did—and I did.

When I first met Kim, I thought she was the most beautiful woman in the world. I was speechless and completely terrified at the idea of going up to talk with her. However, my business training had taught me to overcome my fear of failure and rejection—and that training was about to pay off, big time. Instead of hiding in the back of the room and staring at her from afar, which is exactly what I would have done years earlier, I walked boldly forward and said, "Hi."

Kim turned and flashed her beautiful smile—and I was in love. She was right out of my dreams. But when I asked her out, she said, "No."

An earlier Robert Kiyosaki might have slunk away and admitted defeat. But I had been toughened by my business training: I collected my nerve and asked her out again. Again she said, "No." Now my self-confidence was bruised and my male ego was fading, but I asked her out once again—and again the answer was "No."

This went on for six months. Each time she said, "No," I went into hiding to lick my wounded ego. I was hurting inside. If I had not learned how to overcome my own self-doubts, I could never have kept asking for six months—but I did. And finally, one day, she said, "Yes." We have been together ever since.

I tell this story not just because it's a warm and fuzzy story of how Robert and Kim went a-courting; I tell it because it makes a critical point: This is not just about business and money. This is your *life* we're talking about. How you earn your money and build your career is how you earn your destiny and build your legacy.

Chapter 11

Asset #3: *A Circle of Friends Who Share Your Dreams and Values*

This may be tough to hear, but if you want to create a different economy in your life, you may need to get new friends more than you need to get a new job. Why? Because even though they love you, and even though they don't mean to, the friends you hang with right now might be holding you down.

You may have heard that your income tends to be about equal to the average income of your five closest friends. And you've no doubt heard the saying, "Birds of a feather flock together." That also holds true for rich people, poor people, and middle-class people. In other words, the rich network with the rich, the poor network with other poor people, and the middle class hangs out with the middle class.

My rich dad often said, "If you want to become rich, you need to network with those who are rich or who can help you become rich."

Many people spend their lives hanging out and networking with people who hold them back financially. In a network marketing business, you hang out with people who are there to help you become richer. Ask yourself this: "Are the people with whom I spend time dedicated to me becoming rich? Or are they more interested in me continuing on as a hard worker?"

By the age of 15, I knew that I wanted to become financially free, and that one way to do that was to learn how to network with people who could help me become financially free. I decided I would seek the friendship of friends who were interested in me becoming a rich person, rather than becoming a loyal employee working for the rich.

This was a life-changing moment. It was not an easy decision, because at 15, I had to be very careful about who I spent my time with and which teachers I would listen to. If you are considering building your own business, you need to be acutely aware of who you're spending your time with and who your teachers are. It's a crucial consideration.

The hardest thing about leaving Xerox was that I had to let go of some friendships. Most of my friends and family were in the E quadrant, and they had

CHAPTER 11: *Asset #3:* A Circle of Friends Who Share Your Dreams and Values

different values than I did. They valued security and a steady paycheck, and I valued freedom and financial independence. This made my decision a painful experience, but it was a necessary decision to make if I was going to grow.

You may well experience something similar in network marketing. You may find that there are friends or family members who don't understand or sympathize with your decision to look into network marketing, or who may even actively try to discourage you. You may have friends tell you that you're nuts, you're a sucker, or you're making a huge mistake. You may even lose friends. I hesitate to write that sentence, because it sounds harsh. But that's because it is harsh. It's reality.

And mind you, this has nothing to do with network marketing itself. What's really going on here is that you are making a seismic shift in your life, from living in the E or S quadrant to living in the B quadrant. This is *not* simply taking a different job; it's more like moving to a different country, changing your religion, or switching political parties.

Network marketing not only provides a great business education, it also provides a whole-new world of friends—friends who are going in the same direction as you are and share the same core values as you do.

The English poet John Donne wrote, "No man is an island, entire of itself; every man is a piece of the continent, a part of the main." He said that way back in 1623, and it's a thousand times truer in the incredibly interconnected world of today. You can't get rich in isolation; you are only as good as the community of people you hang out with, talk with, work with, and play with.

John: That's true everywhere in life, but it's especially true and especially relevant in network marketing, because when you build a network marketing business, you actually build around yourself a powerful, brand-new community of friends who are learning the same kinds of values and real-world business skills you are.

This is also one of the great advantages of a network marketing business: Rather than being surrounded by people who are competing with you for that next promotion, here your business is filled with people who are just as committed to your success as you are, because your success is what assures their success. Chances are good that some of them will become your new best friends.

In fact, according to the Direct Selling Association (DSA), a significant number of people who join network marketing companies and stick with them rank *the social network they belong to* as an even higher priority than the income they earn.

There you have it: Network marketing not only provides a great business education, it also provides a whole-new world of friends—friends who are going in the same direction as you are and share the same core values as you do.

To me, the kind of friendship John is talking about is every bit as priceless as the best business training.

Today I have friends in all four quadrants, but my core friends—the ones I really hang out with, the ones whose time means the most to me—are in the B and I quadrants.

And by the way, those friends I left behind at Xerox? They are still great friends today. They will *always* be great friends, because they were there for me at a transitional phase of my life. But for me, it was time to move on. If it is time for you to move on and the B quadrant is calling you, you may want to join a network marketing business and begin to meet new friends.

CHAPTER 12

Asset #4: *The Power of Your Own Network*

One of the first things that intrigued me about this business model when I started looking into it seriously in the 1990s was the simple fact that it used the word *network*. I remembered that my rich dad really respected this term.

Thomas Edison was one of my rich dad's heroes. People today often think of Edison as the inventor of the light bulb, but this is not true. Edison did not invent the light bulb; what he did do was improve it and perfect it. Even more important, he figured how to turn it into a business.

After dropping out of school (because his teachers thought he wasn't smart enough to succeed there), Edison took a job selling candies and magazines on the railroads. Soon, he began printing his own newspaper, and within a year, he had hired a team of boys to sell candies along with his newspaper. He had gone from employee to business owner.

The power is not in the product; the power is in the network. If you want to become rich, the best strategy is to find a way to build a strong, viable, growing network.

Young Edison grew restless selling newspapers, and learned how to send and receive Morse code so he could get a job as a telegraph operator. Soon he was one of the best telegraph operators around—and this is where he learned the secret that would make him a millionaire. As a telegraph operator, he saw what had transformed the invention of the telegraph into such a success: It was the system of lines, poles, skilled people, and relay stations. It was the power of a network.

While Edison is famous for tinkering with the light bulb and perfecting the filament that made the bulb practical, Edison's true stroke of genius was to create a company that strung the electric lines that allowed the light bulb to penetrate society. The company Edison founded would make him a multimillionaire. It was called General Electric.

CHAPTER 12: *Asset #4:* The Power of Your Own Network

What made Edison's business so revolutionary was not the light bulb itself, but the system of electrical lines and relay stations that powered the light bulb. It was the *network*.

My rich dad told me, "The richest people in the world build networks. Everyone else looks for work."

From the shipping magnates and railroad barons to Sam Walton, Bill Gates, and Jeff Bezos, the great fortunes of the world have been made by those who figured out how to build networks. Sam Walton didn't manufacture goods for people; he built the distribution network that delivers the goods. Bill Gates didn't build computers; he built the operating system that ran on those computers. Jeff Bezos didn't go into publishing books; he created the online network Amazon that delivers those books.

The power is not in the product; the power is in the network. If you want to become rich, the best strategy is to find a way to build a strong, viable, growing network.

Of course, most of us are not Thomas Edison, Sam Walton, or Bill Gates, and never will be. Yes, there will be handfuls of remarkably creative pioneers in every generation who create new multibillion-dollar networks from scratch, as these men did, but it's not a reasonable ambition for tens of thousands of people, let alone millions.

That's why network marketing is so brilliant. The companies that make up the network marketing industry now offer millions of people just like yourself the opportunity to build their own network rather than spend their lives working for someone else's network.

Metcalfe's Law

Robert Metcalfe, the founder of 3Com and one of the creators of Ethernet, is credited with creating an equation that defines the value of networks:

$$V = N^2$$

In other words, a network's economic value equals the number of the network's users squared.

Putting Metcalfe's Law in simpler terms, it means that as you add users, its value increases geometrically.

Think of a network of telephones. If you have just one telephone, that single telephone has no real economic value. (If you're the only one with a phone, who would you call?) The moment you add a phone, according to Metcalfe's Law, the economic value of the phone network is squared. The economic value of the network would go from zero to two squared, or four. Add a third phone, and the economic value of the network is now nine. In other words, the economic value of a network goes up exponentially, not numerically.

Networks Come to the Business World

The classic Industrial-Age business model operated much like an empire. It was controlled by a strong central "government" that maintained its strongly centralized identity no matter how big it grew.

In the 1950s, a new type of business emerged, one that maintained its coherence not by controlling all its parts with a single central office, but instead by using the model of a network. This idea was so revolutionary that many criticized it, and the U.S. Congress came within eleven votes of declaring it illegal. But it survived its early years, and today is responsible for more than 3 percent of American retail sales and is thriving around the globe. Some of its more famous brands include Ace Hardware, Subway, and, of course, the most famous of them all, McDonald's.

That radical business model is called a *franchise*.

A franchise is a type of business network in which multiple business owners all work off the same blueprint. In a very pragmatic sense, you could say they all share the same values.

But franchising was just one step in the process of developing networks in the business world. I'll let John tell you what happened next.

John: Robert's right. This isn't just a question of paying a commission differently, or shifting the responsibility of marketing to a different party. It's really an entirely different way of looking at business—one that reflects an Information-Age economy through networking rather than an Industrial-Age economy through centralized mass-advertising.

After franchising, the next step in the development of networked businesses began in the 1960s and really got under way in the 1970s and '80s. Instead of a network of franchised businesses, this model built itself through a network of franchised *individuals*. In a sense, you could call this a "personal franchise."

Like the original franchise model, this new type of business also came under a lot of criticism; yet, despite its critics, it has survived and thrived.

That model is called network marketing.

Robert: And, by the way, the truth about franchising is that as a franchise owner, you are part of a network—but you don't own the network; you own only your particular business. As a network marketer, on the other hand …

John: As a network marketer, you not only build the network, but you actually own your own network. And, as you put it, Robert, that gives you tremendous financial leverage.

In other words, as a network marketer, you get to personally harness the power of Metcalfe's Law.

How? This doesn't happen simply by affiliating with a network marketing company. That's like having a telephone when you are the only one with the telephone. To harness the power of Metcalfe's Law, you have to grow the network

Chapter 12: *Asset #4:* The Power of Your Own Network

by duplicating yourself in someone else just like you: a partner. The moment there are two of you, the economic value of your network is *squared*. When there are three of you, the economic value of your network goes from four to nine. When the two people you brought in also develop two more people each, the economic value of your network begins to look like a rocket taking off for the moon. You are working arithmetically, but your economic value is growing exponentially.

In plain language, Metcalfe's Law means that a network acts as a lever: It allows you to *leverage* your time and effort.

Archimedes, the engineer of ancient Greece credited with discovering the principle of leverage, declared: "Give me a place to stand on, and I can move the world." To demonstrate the virtually limitless power of leverage, he set up an elaborate system of ropes and pulleys, and attached this vast matrix of ropes to an entire fleet of Greek warships. When everything was ready and the crowd watching him grew silent, Archimedes grabbed this one wooden beam and pulled with all his might—and the entire fleet of ships began moving in the water!

That's the power of a network.

Through that matrix of ropes, Archimedes could perform a feat that would normally take the combined strength of several thousand oarsmen. And what exactly *was* that matrix of ropes? A *network*.

That's the phenomenal force that makes rumors spread: One person tells three, who each tell three, who each tell three, and pretty soon everyone in town knows about it. That's how fashion trends spread. And that's the core strategy of a network marketing business: harnessing the power of Metcalf's Law to duplicate your efforts through a network of people.

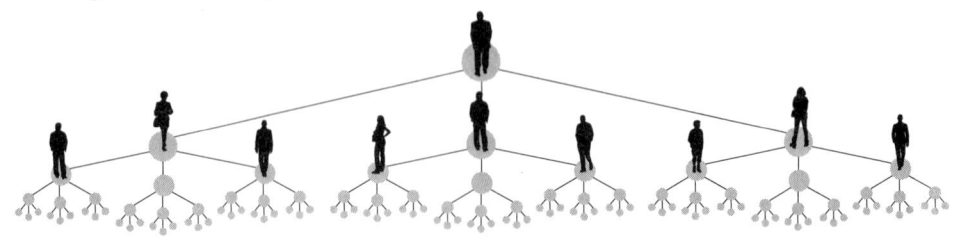

Network marketing is one of the fastest-growing business models in the world today, yet most people still cannot see it. Why not? People might see the product—the home-care or wellness products, or the telecom, financial, or legal services—but they don't realize that that isn't really the business. The real business is not the product, but the networks through which the product travels—not Edison's light bulb, but his electric grid.

People still don't grasp the value of network marketing because it is invisible: It is *virtual*, not material. You cannot see it with your eyes because there is very little to see. It is a genuine Information-Age business model: To grasp its value, it's not enough to open your eyes; you need to open your mind. There are no golden arches, no green mermaids beckoning you to come into their place of business. The business of network marketing has exploded throughout the world, yet the masses often still do not see it.

Businesses such as General Motors and General Electric are Industrial-Age businesses. Franchises—McDonald's, Subway, The UPS Store, Ace Hardware, and the rest—are transition businesses that sprang up to bridge the passage from the Industrial Age into the Information Age. Network marketing businesses are genuine Information-Age businesses, because they deal not with land and materials, factories and employees, but with pure information.

As a network marketer, you might think your job is to demonstrate and sell a product. It's not. Your job is to communicate information, to tell a great story and build a network.

CHAPTER 13

Asset #5: *A Duplicable, Fully Scalable Business*

Here's a critical truth about network marketing that may surprise you: It is not a business for those who are gifted in sales. I promised a few chapters back that John would say more about this, and now's the time.

Robert: John, would you agree that the most successful people in network marketing are not necessarily the best natural salespeople?

John: Not only would I completely agree, but in fact, I would say that, in a way, the *opposite* is true. For a "born salesman" to succeed in network marketing, often the first thing he or she has to do is *forget everything they know about selling*.

Many of the most successful network marketers I've ever seen have been coaches, moms, pastors, teachers—people who really enjoy telling stories and helping others. Network marketing is about sharing information and personal stories, and not about hard selling. It is also about *caring* about the success of those you bring into the business.

Which is a good thing, by the way, because only one person in twenty is a natural-born salesman anyway.

The key to success in sales is what you can do.

The key to success in network marketing is what you can *duplicate*.

Robert: Sometimes when I say that this business is not about sales, I get a skeptical reaction. "Yeah, but aren't you kind of splitting hairs? I mean, whether you call it *selling* or *sharing information*, isn't it pretty much semantics?"

John: No, it's not semantics, and you're not splitting hairs. And it's that duplication factor that really dramatically shows you the huge difference between sales and network marketing.

Here's what I would tell that person:

"If you are an amazing, uniquely skilled, superstar salesperson, then you can do great in sales—and chances are good, you will do lousy in network marketing."

Chapter 13: *Asset #5:* A Duplicable, Fully Scalable Business

Why? Because while you might sell a lot of products, *most people in your network won't be able to duplicate what you do.* Consequently, your network cannot grow, and it dies an early death.

Robert: Because you smothered it in the cradle.

John: That's right, and I've seen it happen many times. I often watch talented and creative people start out in network marketing and run into this brick wall because they think that the way to be successful is to use their ingenuity, talent, and unique skills to be amazing. But it's not a question of what you can do; it's what you can do and then what *others* can do, too.

I have also seen companies make the mistake of too strongly recognizing high levels of personal sales as opposed to placing more emphasis on showing everyone how to duplicate their efforts in the performance of others. The ability to duplicate is the magic key here, not the ability to be a top salesperson. When network marketing companies fail to make this clear, they impair their ability to continuously develop and energize their growth engine: the people who duplicate themselves.

Robert: That's fascinating, because when you talk about people who try to be ingenious about it, you know what that is? That's thinking like a person in the S quadrant—not in the B quadrant. When you live in the S quadrant, then, by all means, be brilliant and creative and unique! But in the B quadrant? Kiss of death.

Henry Ford did not create an empire and change the face of the planet by building a business model around his workers' unique skills and talents.

Now, he *could* have hired craftsmen to hand-make his cars. They would have been amazing cars—and he would have sold maybe a few hundred of them. Instead, he designed a model where ordinary people could plug in their time and effort and mass-produce millions of cars.

Ford thought like a person who lived smack in the B quadrant.

John: I wouldn't have thought of putting it that way, but that's exactly what it is. And if you want to be successful in network marketing, that's how *you* have to think.

Again, what gives your network marketing business its real power is not what *you* can do; it's what you can *duplicate*. In other words, you want to build your business in a way that virtually anyone else can readily copy. Why? Because others copying what you do is exactly what you want to happen—what you *need* to have happen. That's what creates your success.

We'll rejoin this discussion of duplication in a moment, but first I want to talk a little about that term *scalable*.

Information Tools for Infinite Scalability

Another way of saying what John is talking about, when he says the secret is duplication, is this: The power of your business is in its *scalability*. A business that is *scalable* simply means a business that can operate on any scale.

This is often the make-or-break issue with entrepreneurs. The world is full of would-be entrepreneurs who create businesses that are wonderful, as long as they're operating on a scale so small that they can personally control every aspect of the business. But there are very few entrepreneurs who grasp how to design their tiny little business model so it can be multiplied and replicated many times over *without their direct participation.*

This is the secret of Ray Kroc's brilliance in creating the McDonald's phenomenon. He didn't seek out an elite corps of especially talented restaurateurs with high-level expertise to run his multiple operations. Instead, *he designed the expertise right into the operation.*

That's exactly what smart network marketing companies have done. Instead of trying to recruit only the most highly skilled speakers, presenters, and salespeople, they have designed the presenting into the system itself, in the form of *information tools*—and as John explains it, that didn't happen overnight.

John: In the early days of network marketing, its practitioners faced a thorny challenge: While it is true that anyone can learn to give a presentation, it is not true that just anyone can give an *effective* presentation. This meant that, while theoretically "anyone" could be successful in this business, it often wasn't that way in reality.

In the early days, the business really did rely on people with great presentation skills, and a big part of learning the business was learning how to make a great presentation. But just as with sales, very few people are ever going to get truly skilled at making a polished, professional presentation. So this put a serious limitation on the business's ability to grow.

Robert: And that's where presentation tools come into the picture.

John: That's right. Years ago, people tried to do this with brochures and sales books, and they had a degree of success. While the average person might not be able to become a great presenter, he or she could walk a prospect through a brochure or catalog. But brochures and booklets are simply not engaging enough to capture someone's interest in the way a great live presentation from a dynamic presenter can.

Over the past few decades, though, there has been a seismic shift in presentation technology. The explosion of digital technology has leveled the playing field. Digital tools—CDs, DVDs, and online media—have now made it possible to recreate that fully engaging, dynamic quality of a live presentation.

I find it interesting that you're calling this book *The Business of the 21st Century*, Robert, because even though it has been around for decades, in a very real way, this business model is just now coming into its real potential—and what we're talking about right now is one of the reasons why.

Chapter 13: *Asset #5:* A Duplicable, Fully Scalable Business

Today, when you start your own network marketing business, you don't *have* to become an adept public speaker. In fact, trying to be one can actually work against you, because again, that's a highly specialized skill, and therefore not very duplicable.

Instead of attempting to train yourself to become an expert speaker and presenter, you simply use the business tools provided by your company to *do the presentations for you.*

What's more, these business tools are highly affordable, both because it is in the companies' interest to *make* them affordable, and also because technology has now made it possible.

Low-cost, high-quality CDs, DVDs, and online presentations—often including high-quality streaming audio and video—have made possible the dream of a truly democratic *and fully scalable* network marketing operation, creating a business model that has allowed millions to gain access and excel.

Do you realize what this means? It means that as you build your networking business, you are building a fully scalable asset. In plain English, it means you can grow a business as big as you want.

Before we go on, though, I have to play the devil's advocate one more time.

Robert: John, I have to ask you the question I've heard skeptics ask when they hear this point about being duplicable:

"So if you don't really have to be a top salesperson, and you don't have to be an expert speaker or presenter, what do you do? Why does the company even need you?"

John: You network. That's why it's called network marketing, and that's why the company needs you—and why they pay you.

As a network marketer, your job description, so to speak, is to connect with people, invite them to experience the products you are excited about and take a look at the information you have, and then follow up with them. Then, once they've decided to join you in the business, you share with them your enthusiasm, your experiences, and you help them learn to do what you have learned to do. Here, again, there are digital tools that can take a huge amount of the burden and expertise of training off your shoulders.

Your job is to build relationships, have conversations, explore possibilities, get to know people, and help them get to understand what this business is all about.

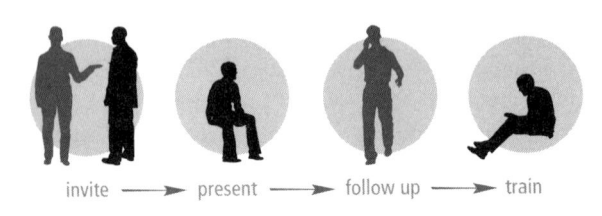

invite ⟶ present ⟶ follow up ⟶ train

So there are parts of this business that a tool can do better than you can: That's the presentation, and to an extent, the training. And there are parts that only you can uniquely do, and that's the human connection part.

Here is the core idea: In network marketing, *you are the messenger, not the message.*

Gone are the days of carting around a heavy pack of products to sample, setting up an entire retail store in your living room, or having to memorize long lists of product features and financial statistics. *This is the 21st century.* In today's network marketing, the tools do all that. Your job is to connect and invite.

And by the way, this doesn't mean you don't need to be skilled. You absolutely do. You need to develop the skills we looked at as part of Asset #1: the ability to have self-confidence, withstand rejection, communicate, be a great storyteller, care about people, coach people, and the rest.

But these are skills available to anyone. If you've ever helped build a soccer league, PTA group, or chess club, ever been part of a political campaign or church committee, ever coached Little League or formed your own band, then you know what it's like to build a network.

You don't need highly skilled salespeople to duplicate what you do. You need people who are willing to learn basic business and communication skills and grow themselves personally into self-determining entrepreneurs and team-builders.

Very few people are truly skilled at sales. But practically anyone can become skilled at networking, coaching, and team-building. Which means this business is open for business to hundreds of millions of your neighbors. Which means you have a readily duplicable, fully scalable business. Once you've grown it to five people and then fifty, you've mastered the basic skills it takes to grow it to five hundred, five thousand, and beyond.

Which brings us to *leadership*.

CHAPTER 14

Asset #6: *Incomparable Leadership Skills*

When I was first researching the world of network marketing, I went to many meetings and events where I heard dozens of people speaking from the front of the room in their efforts to inspire others to find their own personal greatness.

As I listened to these individuals tell their stories of starting with nothing and eventually becoming wealthy beyond their wildest dreams, I realized that this business was doing for these people exactly what my rich dad told me to do: It wasn't simply teaching them the principles of business; it was shaping them into leaders.

While they seemed to be talking a lot about money, these people were really inspiring others to get out of their shells, go beyond their fears, and go for their dreams. To do that required leadership skills on the part of the speaker. The reason it takes leadership is that while many people repeat the same overused words and phrases about *dreams, more time with family,* and *freedom,* few people inspire enough trust and inspiration to cause others to follow those words and phrases.

It's not a matter of memorizing and repeating the right words; it's developing the ability to speak directly to other people's spirits. This is a quality that goes beyond words. This is genuine leadership.

Leadership is the force that makes it all come together. Leadership is what builds great businesses.

You might think that leadership skills would be included as part of Asset #1, "A Real-World Business Education," or Asset #2, "A Profitable Path of Personal Development." That's reasonable; you could make a case for both. But the truth is, having the capacity to lead is a skill set so valuable, so powerful, and so rare that it is genuinely an asset unto itself, and deserves its own chapter.

All the other business skills are important ingredients. Leadership is the force that makes it all come together. Leadership is what builds great businesses.

CHAPTER 14: *Asset #6:* Incomparable Leadership Skills

Speaking Directly to Spirit

I grew up in the '50s and '60s, and John F. Kennedy was one of the greatest speakers I have ever heard. When he told the nation in May 1961 that we were going to put a man on the moon *within the decade*, our scientists really didn't have a clue how we could possibly accomplish such a thing. It was beyond ambitious; it was outrageous. And yet we did it. Even though JFK was killed less than three years later, with three-quarters of the decade left to go, his leadership was so compelling and so powerful that his vision persisted after his death. Despite his assassination, despite the catastrophe of Vietnam, despite the nation being rocked by riots and division and the presidential mantle passing from JFK's vice president to his former rival Richard Nixon in 1968, what did we do?

We put a man on the moon in 1969—sure enough, *within the decade*.

That's leadership: the power to make things happen through the sheer force of the vision you share. Genuine leaders can move mountains.

In Vietnam, I discovered that great leaders were not tough people who yelled and screamed or were physically abusive. In the heat of battle, I found that great, brave leaders were often quiet, yet when they spoke, they spoke to our souls and our spirits.

Money does not go to the business with the best products or service. Money flows to the business with the best leaders.

All great leaders have been master storytellers who were able to communicate the vision in such a vivid way that others saw it, too. Look at Jesus Christ, Buddha, Mother Teresa, Gandhi, Muhammad. They were all great leaders, which means they were great storytellers.

Money does not go to the business with the best products or service. Money flows to the business with the best leaders. A business that has forgotten how to tell its own story is soon *out* of business, even if it has tons of inventory. When I find a business that is struggling financially, it is often because the leader of that business cannot communicate the company's vision—he or she cannot tell the story. They may be smart, but they are poor communicators.

The leadership skills you need to develop for the B quadrant are very different from the management skills most often required for the E and S quadrants. Don't get me wrong: Management skills are important, but there is a vast difference between management skills and leadership skills. Managers are not necessarily leaders, and leaders are not necessarily managers.

I meet many people in the S quadrant, the specialists or small-business owners, who would like to expand their businesses but cannot, for one reason: They lack leadership skills. No one wants to follow them. Their employees do not trust them, are not inspired by them. I have met many middle managers who fail to climb the corporate ladder because they cannot communicate with others. The world is full of lonely people who cannot seem to find the man or woman of their dreams, simply because they fail to communicate what a good person they are.

Communication affects every aspect of life—and this is the No. 1 skill that network marketing teaches.

Network marketing leaders sometimes describe themselves as "highly paid storytellers." In fact, they are among the *most* highly paid storytellers, and there's a very simple reason for this: They are among the *best* storytellers.

When I started attending network marketing business trainings, I got to meet highly successful, real-world business owners who had started their businesses from scratch. Many were great teachers because they were teaching from experience and not from theory. Sitting through many of the business seminars, I often found myself nodding in agreement with their straight talk about what it takes to survive on the streets of the real world of business.

After the seminars, I would often talk to the instructors. I was amazed at how much money they made, not only from their businesses, but also from their investments. Several made significantly more than many top CEOs in corporate America.

Yet, there was something else to these instructors that impressed me even more. Although they were rich and certainly did not *have* to be leading these events, they had a passion for teaching and helping their fellow human beings.

I began to realize that a network marketing business is based on the leaders pulling people up, while a traditional corporate or government business is based on promoting only a few and keeping the masses of employees content with a steady paycheck. These instructors in the network marketing world were *not* saying, "If you don't perform, you lose your job." Instead, they were saying, "Let me help you do better and better. As long as you want to learn, I'll be here to teach you. We're on the same team."

A Very Special Type of Leader

Many people have leadership qualities within them, but these qualities are never brought out. They never have the opportunity. My rich dad understood this. One reason he encouraged me to go into the Marine Corps and then on to Vietnam was that it would develop my leadership skills.

But you don't need to join the Marines to have the chance for the leader within you to blossom. You can have that chance through network marketing. And the real beauty of a network marketing leadership program is not simply the fact that it develops leadership, but the particular *type* of leadership it brings out.

Network marketing tends to develop the type of leader who influences others by being a great teacher, teaching others to fulfill their life's dreams by teaching others to go for *their* dreams.

The military develops a type of leader who inspires men and women to defend their country. The world of business develops a type of leader who builds teams to beat the competition. Network marketing tends to develop the type of leader who influences others by being a great teacher, teaching others to fulfill their life's dreams by teaching others to go for *their* dreams.

CHAPTER 14: *Asset #6:* Incomparable Leadership Skills

Instead of beating the enemy or beating the competition, most network marketing leaders simply inspire and teach others to find the financial bounty this world offers without harm to others.

The opportunity to develop the capacity to lead is a value uniquely intrinsic to network marketing. Sure, you could learn leadership in any other field. From the military to government to corporate life, every sphere of life produces leaders, but not very many. Genuine leadership is extremely rare—except in network marketing.

John has an interesting perspective on why this is so.

John: What is unique about network marketing is that it marries a broad compensation structure to a field of people made up of 100 percent of volunteers.

You will not find a single network marketing distributor who punches a time clock or *has* to show up for work. As independent representatives, no one is hired or fired—everyone is there voluntarily. Nobody can tell you what to do; no one can give you orders.

So why does it work? What's the engine that drives the machine? The answer comes in one word: leadership.

And the leadership you develop in your network marketing business will show up in every other sphere of your life.

The Four Elements of Leadership

Traditional schools train you to be a good employee. They focus on one thing only: your mental ability. If you can solve equations and do well on tests, then you're considered smart enough to run a company.

That's ridiculous.

The reason I am a successful entrepreneur today is because of the training I received in the Marines. Military schools prepare you to be a great leader by focusing not only on your mind, but also on your emotional, physical, and spiritual abilities. They teach you how to operate under extreme pressure.

I had the smarts to fly a helicopter in Vietnam, but I never would have made it back without the development of my spirituality. If that had not been strong, then fear (emotion) would have set in, and I would very likely have frozen up (physical) at the controls of the gunship. Having these four elements—mental, emotional, physical, and spiritual—working in harmony helped me make it through my missions.

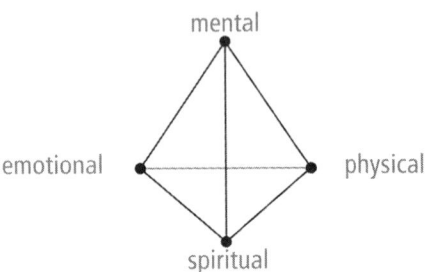

This also armed me with the knowledge and understanding it took to be a good leader in the business world, because these are exactly the same four elements of leadership required to be successful in business. Mind; spirit; body; emotions:

If you cannot control these four aspects of yourself, then you will fail. And if you are not able to help develop these four elements in your employees, and in so doing help them to become effective leaders, then you will fail. It's as simple as that.

Here's another thing military schools teach you: Being on the front lines means not caring about whether or not you are liked. Of course, we all *want* to be liked—but to be a great leader, you have to set boundaries, monitor the behavior of your staff, and take corrective action when necessary. Sometimes you're going to tick people off. Yes, it's going to happen—there's no way around it. But here is what's also going to happen: You are going to create the best team possible, one that understands what you expect, and what you will and will not tolerate.

CHAPTER 15

Asset #7: *A Mechanism for Genuine Wealth Creation*

Thomas Jefferson and John Adams, two of the three creators of the Declaration of Independence, were great lifelong friends, although their friendship was not without differences, even huge ones. They were temperamental opposites, and at one point they became bitter political arch-rivals, diametrically opposed on many issues. For years, our second and third presidents refused to speak with one another. But in their later years they reconciled, and their lengthy correspondence is one of the great treasures of American literature.

They died on the very same day, on July 4, 1826—fifty years to the day from the signing of the Declaration of Independence that they had co-authored with Benjamin Franklin.

There is one more curious fact about these two men: their relationship to wealth.

Jefferson was the classic Virginia aristocratic landowner, possessing an estate encompassing thousands of acres. Adams was a Massachusetts barrister from a fairly poor farm family, and lived his long life without ever having much in the way of wealth. And yet, on the day of their death, Adams was worth about $100,000—and Jefferson's estate was about $100,000 in *debt*.

> **Wealth is not the same thing as money. Wealth is not measured by the size of income. Wealth is measured in time.**

Jefferson had money and property, but it slipped through his fingers. Adams never had much *money*, but though he lived simply, he had a firm grasp on how to build wealth.

One of the central reasons I'm writing this book is to make sure you grasp the crucial difference between money and wealth. Why does the typical million-dollar lottery winner end up broke within three years after earning his or her millions? Because while they had a sudden windfall of *money*, they had no concept of *wealth*.

CHAPTER 15: *Asset #7:* A Mechanism for Genuine Wealth Creation

Wealth is not the same thing as money. Wealth is not measured by the size of income. Wealth is measured in time. If all I have to my name is $1,000 in savings and checking combined, and my living expenses are $100 a day, then my wealth equals ten days. Wealth is the ability to survive so many number of days forward. Ask yourself, "If I stop working today, how long could I survive financially?" Your answer is equal to your wealth at this moment.

Actually, let's deepen that definition. Wealth is measured by *the richness of your life experience today plus the number of days into the future* that you have the capacity to continue living at that level of experience.

One reason the rich get richer is that the rich work for a different kind of money. They don't work to generate income—they work to build wealth. There is a vast difference between the two.

One of the most profound values of a network marketing business—and it is one that the great majority of people who look at this business do not quite grasp—is that it is an engine of personal wealth creation.

My Simple Four-Step Path to Financial Freedom

Kim and I were able to retire early in life without jobs, without government assistance, and without any trading of stocks or any mutual funds. Why no trading of stocks or mutual funds? Because we believed they were very risky investments. In my opinion, mutual funds are some of the riskiest of all investments.

Kim and I used a simple four-step plan to retire young and rich. It took us nine years, from 1985 to 1994, starting with nothing and retiring financially free—without a single share of stock or mutual funds. It goes like this:

1) Build a business
2) Reinvest in your business
3) Invest in real estate
4) Let your assets buy luxuries

Let's look at how this sequence works.

1) Build a Business

Building a business allows you to generate a lot of money. Furthermore, the tax laws of the United States are very favorable to people who earn their income in the B quadrant and punish people who earn their money in the E quadrant.

A business is like a child: It takes time to grow. While it can take less time, and can certainly take more, getting a business off the ground typically takes about five years.

2) Reinvest in Your Business

The key to this process is that you don't try to use your business as an income source to live on. A lot of first-time network marketers make this mistake. As soon as they start seeing an income stream develop from their new business, they use that new income to expand their living expenses: buy a second car, buy a bigger house, take expensive vacations, and so forth.

Why do people do this? It's not because they're idiots: I've seen very intelligent, well-informed people follow this pattern. They do it for one reason and one reason only: They are still living, breathing, and thinking *in the E quadrant*. If you want to build wealth, you have to get your head out of the left-hand side of that diagram and start thinking *B* and *I*.

First, keep your day job. Your goal is not to replace your job with your business—that's just treating your business like your new job. You'll never build wealth that way. Instead, once your new business is making some money, go right to Step 2: Reinvest your new income in that business in order to grow it still further.

"But I don't want to keep my day job—I hate working there! Isn't that the whole point? I want to stop working as an employee!"

The reason so many people fail to achieve great wealth in any business is simply that they fail to reinvest continually in the business.

Fair enough: You want to get out of the E quadrant and quit that job. Maybe you hate your job. Or you may be like a lot of professionals I've met who actually love what they do, but don't love the fact that they *have* to keep doing it forty, fifty or sixty hours a week. Whatever your reasons, here's the blunt truth: If you suck all the income out of your new business to burn on monthly living expenses, then you're not building a business; you're just building yourself another job.

A true business owner never stops investing and reinvesting to build the business. The reason so many people fail to achieve great wealth in any business is simply that they fail to reinvest continually in the business.

So, what does that look like in network marketing?

John: A traditional business might reinvest by building a new warehouse, spending money on national advertising, developing new product lines, or buying new distribution channels. But as a network marketer, you don't have these expenses: The network marketing company itself makes these types of investments for you.

How *do* you reinvest in your business, then? There are certainly places where you can invest some money wisely: on training and educating yourself, on travel to support your growing network in other cities, on promotional and educational tools and resources to help nourish the business.

CHAPTER 15: *Asset #7: A Mechanism for Genuine Wealth Creation*

For the most part, though, network marketing is a business whose major capital investment is not your money but your *time and effort*.

Which means the better part of your networking income becomes available to you to feed the serious process of building your wealth. But notice, I did say "building your wealth," not "squandering your wealth"!

Don't make the mistake I've seen people make, and start spending every last dollar from your new commission checks on a bigger car, bigger house, bigger lifestyle. Don't abuse your new business income by pouring it into bigger holes in the ground.

Treat it with the respect it deserves. Invest it.

3) Invest in Real Estate

As your business income continues to grow, you begin using that supplemental income to buy real estate.

You'll notice there are no mutual funds, stock portfolios, or other paper assets in this plan. That's because even though they are the easiest assets to build (all you have to do is buy them), trading in stocks and mutual funds is risky, profits made are taxed at the capital gain rate, and investing takes financial education to lessen risk. The idea here is to use your new supplemental money to build an income-generating asset. There are many types of assets that can generate income, but the one I recommend most often is real estate, for two principal reasons.

First, the tax laws are written in favor of business owners who invest in real estate.

Second, your banker loves to lend you money for real estate. Try asking your banker for a thirty-year loan at 6.5 percent to buy mutual funds or stocks. They'll laugh you out of the bank.

People often ask me, "How can I buy real estate when I barely earn enough money to pay the rent?" Good question; you can't. Not, that is, until you have the extra cash. That's why this step comes *after* building a business and reinvesting in its continued growth: so you have the extra cash.

But let me explain what I mean when I say, "Invest in real estate," because many people completely misunderstand how real estate works as an asset. Most people think that the point of real estate is to buy a property at one price and then sell it (either quickly, after some hasty improvements, or at a later time) for a higher price. Wrong. That's just buying a cow and then selling it for steaks. What you want to do is buy a cow and keep it forever so you can sell its milk.

The purpose of buying real estate is not to sell it; the purpose of buying real estate is to build an income-generating asset.

Learning how to do this takes time, education, experience, and money. As with learning anything new, it's difficult not to make some mistakes—and mistakes in real estate (especially in property management) can be very expensive. Unless you have the extra steady income and the tax advantages that come with a B quadrant business, real estate is either too risky or too slow.

The reason many people fail to become rich in real estate is that they don't have the cash it takes. The truth is, the best real estate deals are usually expensive. If you don't have much money, often the only real estate deals you can get are deals that people with real money have passed on. The reason so many people try looking for "no money down" investments is that they have nothing to put down! Unless you are really experienced and have plenty of cash on hand to use when you need it, putting nothing down could be the most expensive investment of your life.

4) Let Your Assets Buy Luxuries

For many years, even long after we could have afforded to do more, Kim and I continued to live in a small house with a monthly mortgage of about $400 and drove average cars. Meanwhile, we were using whatever extra cash we generated to build our business and invest in real estate.

Today we live in a large home and have six luxury cars between us—but we didn't buy that house or those cars. Our *assets* bought them; we just enjoy them.

When I say "luxury," I don't necessarily mean something extravagant or ostentatious. I mean something that you want and enjoy, and that exists beyond what you "need."

I'll give you an example. Think of anyone you know who works for a living but does not love their job. If you told them—"Hey, you don't like your job, you should just quit!"—what would they say?

I'd love to—but I don't have that luxury.

That's right: For many people, simply not having their job is one of the very first luxuries they want. How do you get that luxury? The same as any other: You let your business and/or your real estate holdings buy it for you. For that to happen, you have to build those assets to the point where they *can* buy it for you.

You see how it works?

You don't use your income to buy yourself luxuries: You use your income to build your assets—your business and real estate investments—and then, once they're sufficiently built to be able to do so, you let *them* buy your luxuries.

Which brings us to the matter of dreams.

CHAPTER 16

Asset #8: *Big Dreams and the Capacity to Live Them*

One of the most valuable things about network marketing companies is that they stress the importance of going for your dreams. Notice, I didn't say "the importance of *having* dreams." They don't just want you to *have* dreams; they want you to *live* those dreams.

What's more, they encourage you to dream *big*. One of the most refreshing things that happened to me when I started looking into network marketing was that I found myself dreaming even bigger dreams than I already had.

Traditional businesses are often not too keen on you having big dreams. They operate better if you have modest dreams: a brief summer vacation, maybe a small time share, a hobby you enjoy, a good game of golf on a Sunday afternoon. That kind of thing.

I'm not saying there's anything wrong with having such small dreams. All I'm saying is, that's a small life.

Growing up, I often heard my parents use the phrase, "We can't afford it." My rich dad, however, forbade his son and me from saying those words, and insisted instead that we ask ourselves, "*How* can I afford it?"

As small as the difference between those statements may seem, it makes all the difference. That small shift in thinking, multiplied by the experiences, perceptions, and decisions of a lifetime, will take you to a place that is millions of miles away from where you would have landed without that shift.

When you make a habit of asking yourself, "*How* can I afford that?" you train yourself to dream bigger and bigger dreams, and not only to have those dreams but to believe that you can make them come true. Saying "I can't afford that," on the other hand, snuffs out your dreams like a wet towel on a candle flame. There are already plenty of other people in the world who try to smother your dreams, without you adding your voice to the mix! Oh, they don't mean to, perhaps, but well-meaning or not, their words are deadly.

CHAPTER 16: *Asset #8:* Big Dreams and the Capacity to Live Them

"You can't do that."

"That's too risky. Do you know how many people have failed trying to do that?"

"Don't be silly. Where do you come up with such ideas?"

"If it's such a good idea, wouldn't someone else have already done it?"

"Oh, I tried that years ago. Let me tell you why it won't work."

These are dream-killing words, and I've noticed something interesting about the people who say them: They are almost always people who have already given up on their own dreams.

It is striving, learning, and doing your best to develop your personal power to be able to afford the big house and who you become in the process that are important.

When Kim and I were broke, we told each other that when we had made over $1 million, we would buy a big house. We did, and we loved being in the house, but the house itself was not important to us, and even being able to afford the house was not important to us. What was important was *who we became* in the process.

It is striving, learning, and doing your best to develop your personal power to be able to afford the big house and who you become in the process that are important.

"People who dream small dreams," my rich dad told me, "continue to live lives as small people."

Everyone has dreams, but not everyone dreams in the same way. My rich dad taught me that there are five kinds of dreamers:

- Those who dream in the past
- Those who dream only small dreams
- Those who achieve a dream, and then live bored
- Those who dream big dreams, but with no plan on how to go about achieving them, so end up with nothing
- Those who dream big, achieve those dreams, and go on to dream even bigger dreams!

Those Who Dream in the Past

These are the people who believe that their greatest achievements are behind them. They will regale you with stories of their college days, their army days, their high-school football days, their life on the farm where they grew up; but try to engage them in a conversation about the future, and they'll probably just shake their heads and say, "Ahh, the world's gone to hell in a handbasket."

A person who dreams in the past is a person whose life is over. They may not be dead, but they are no longer truly alive—and the only way they can come back to life is to rekindle a dream.

Those Who Dream Only Small Dreams

Some people limit themselves to dreaming only small dreams, because that's the only way they can feel confident they can achieve them. The ironic thing is that, while they know they could achieve their small dreams, they often never do. Why not? Who knows? Perhaps it's because they know that if they did achieve them, they would have nothing left to live for—unless they then challenged themselves to come up with larger dreams.

In other words, they would rather live small than face the risks and thrill of living large. Later in life, you'll hear them say, "You know, I should have done that years ago, but I just never got around to doing it."

I once asked a man I had met, "If you had all the money in the world, where would you travel?"

He replied, "I would fly to California to visit my sister. I haven't seen her in fourteen years, and I would love to see her, especially before her children get any older. That would be my dream vacation."

At the time, that trip would have cost him about $500. I pointed that out, and asked why he had not yet taken the trip. He told me, "Oh, I will, I'm just too busy right now." In other words, this was the "dream vacation" that he would rather dream about taking than actually wake up and take.

My rich dad told me that these dreamers are often the most dangerous.

"They live like turtles," he said, "tucked away in their own quiet, padded room. If you knock on the shell and peek in, they might lunge out and bite you."

The lesson: Let dreaming turtles dream. Most aren't going anywhere, and that seems to be just fine with them.

Those Who Achieve a Dream, and Then Live Bored

A friend of mine once said to me, "Twenty years ago, I dreamed of becoming a doctor. So I became a doctor. And I enjoy being a doctor, but now I'm bored with life. Something is missing."

Boredom usually is a sign that it's time for a new dream. My rich dad told me, "There are a lot of people who work in professions they dreamed of in high school. The problem is, they've been out of high school for years. It's time for a new adventure."

CHAPTER 16: *Asset #8:* Big Dreams and the Capacity to Live Them

Those Who Dream Big Dreams, But with No Plan on How to Go About Achieving Them, So They End Up with Nothing

I think we all know someone in this category. These people say, "I've just had a major breakthrough. Let me tell you about my new plan." Or, "This time things will be different." Or, "I'm turning over a new leaf." Or, "I'm going to work harder, pay off my bills, and invest." Or, "I just heard of a new company coming to town, and it is looking for someone with my qualifications. This could be my big break."

My rich dad said, "People like this often try to achieve a lot, but they try to do it on their own. But very few people achieve their dreams on their own. These people should keep dreaming big, make a plan, and then find a team that will help them make their dreams come true."

Those Who Dream Big, Achieve Those Dreams, and Go On to Dream Even Bigger Dreams!

I think that most of us would like to be this kind of person. I know I would. Wouldn't you?

My rich dad said it this way: "Big people have big dreams and small people have small dreams. If you want to change who you are, begin by changing the size of your dream."

As you know, I've been broke—totally, flat-out broke, living in my car with my bride. I know what it's like. But *broke* is a temporary condition. Poor is different. Poor is a state of mind. You can be broke and still be rich in spirit, rich in ambition, rich in courage, rich in determination. It costs nothing to dream big, and it costs not one cent more to dream *huge*. No matter how broke you might be, the only way you will become poor is by giving up on your dreams.

The unique thing about the network marketing lifestyle is that you don't frame your dreams as something you reach only after forty years, or only for a few weeks out of the calendar, or only on Sunday afternoons. When you start building your network marketing business, you start living your dreams, albeit in small ways at first, from Day One.

It is a shift in mindset, from "I can't" to "I can"; from being at the mercy of circumstance to being at the helm of your life; from being enslaved to being free.

In his conclusion to *Walden*, his meditation on the self-determined life, Thoreau wrote:

> *I learned this, at least, by my experiment: that if one advances confidently in the direction of his dreams, and endeavors to live the life which he has imagined, he will meet with a success unexpected in common hours.*

I couldn't have said it better myself.

CHAPTER 17

A Business Where Women Excel
by Kim Kiyosaki

By now, you've heard me refer to my wife, Kim, quite a few times; you've read about how we met and how I pursued her, about our early struggles, our goals and our strategies, and how our life together has turned out. Before closing this part of the book, I thought it was high time you had the chance to hear from Kim directly. —R.K.

Robert has told you quite a bit about network marketing and the many ways it can create great value for you. I want to tell you about one more: It is a powerful business for women.

When you look at the basic statistical profile of the network marketing community, one of the first things you notice is also one of the most remarkable: *It is populated by more than four times as many women as men.*

You heard me right. According to the Direct Selling Association, of the fifteen million people in the United States who are in network marketing, about 88 percent are female. And while they do not provide a breakdown by gender of the more than sixty-two million people in the business worldwide, the proportions on a global scale are probably close to the same as in the States.

The supporting, coaching, nurturing relationship of a network marketing sponsor to her growing network of apprentice networkers is the kind of relationship and interaction in which women excel.

Why? Historically, one reason is that many households have started their network marketing businesses as part-time ventures, and for families where the man

CHAPTER 17: A Business Where Women Excel

is the primary breadwinner, that has often meant it was the woman who engaged in the part-time, stay-at-home business.

A parallel factor is the fact that it is a home-based business, which means that building a network marketing business is uniquely compatible with the demands of raising a family.

But I think it goes beyond these practical and historical circumstances.

Network marketing is, at its core, a *relationship* business. As Robert has explained, it's not a business that revolves around making *sales*; it is a business that revolves around making *connections*. It's about establishing relationships, coaching and training, and teaching and mentoring. The actual day-to-day work of building a network is less like carving out a sales territory than it is like building a community.

And the supporting, coaching, nurturing relationship of a network marketing sponsor to her growing network of apprentice networkers is the kind of relationship and interaction in which women excel.

Of course, none of this means that men can't be successful in network marketing, too. There are millions of men who are proving that every day. But the bottom line of the business is simply this: It is a business model where women excel.

What Women Need

And it's a good thing, too, because today's women really need to learn how to build their own wealth.

A young journalist approached me a few years ago and said, with obvious passion, "We have to make women aware that they have to take charge of their money. They cannot depend on someone else to do that for them!"

As we talked together, I soon learned where her passion was coming from. It turned out her 54-year-old mother had recently moved in with her after going through a divorce that had left her with basically nothing. She was now supporting her mother as well as herself.

That was enough of a wake-up call in itself, but what had really shaken her up was when she took a close look at her finances to see what resources she had to support the two of them. She realized that if her steady paycheck were for any reason to stop suddenly, the only thing she had to fall back on was about $7,000 in savings.

For a household of two, $7,000 wouldn't go very far. She and her mom were both a few thin paychecks away from poverty and even homelessness. No wonder she was passionate about the subject of women taking control of their finances!

Fortunately for me, I am not in this young woman's position. Robert and I are financially set for the rest of our lives, regardless of what the economy does.

But even though I don't have that sword hanging over my head, I am just as passionately driven as this young woman was on the subject of women creating their own financial independence.

The "how-to's" of network marketing are no different for women as they are for men. However, the driving reasons *why* women build their network marketing businesses are often very different from those of their male counterparts.

We know that we lead very different lives than our mothers did, but you may be surprised at just how different. Here are six reasons why women need to get into this game called wealth-building.

1) The Statistics

The statistics about women and money are startling. The following are U.S. statistics, yet for other countries throughout the world, the statistics are very similar or are trending in the same direction.

In the United States:

- 47 percent of women over the age of 50 are single; in other words, they are financially responsible for themselves.
- Women's retirement income is less than that of men because as the primary caretaker for the home, a woman is away from the work force an average of 14.7 years, as compared to 1.6 years for men. Add this fact to the lower salaries women still receive, and you have retirement benefits that are only about one-quarter those of men. *(National Center for Women and Retirement Research—NCWRR)*
- Women are expected to live an average of seven to ten years longer than men *(Ann Letteeresee, June 12, 2000)*, which means they must provide for those extra years. However, married women who are baby boomers can expect to outlive their husbands by fifteen to twenty years, on average.
- Of the elderly living in poverty, three out of four are women. *(Morningstar Fund Investor)*
- Approximately seven out of ten women will at some time live in poverty.

What do these statistics tell us? That more and more women are not educated or prepared to take care of themselves financially, especially as they grow older. We've spent our entire lives taking care of our families, but have no ability to care for ourselves in this vital way.

2) Avoiding Dependency

You don't get into a marriage expecting a divorce. You don't begin a new job expecting to be laid off. But it happens, and today with more and more frequency.

Women, if you are depending on a husband, a boss, or anyone else for your financial future, think twice. They may simply not be there. Too often, we may not even realize just how dependent we are until we're faced with our own personal wake-up call.

3) No Glass Ceiling

Along with all the challenges facing the corporate employee in this post-2009 world, women still face one additional, huge obstacle: the infamous "glass ceiling."

Chapter 17: A Business Where Women Excel

Yes, it's true, even today: Because of our gender, women can move only so far up the corporate ladder. And for women 50 or older, trying to re-enter the world of corporate employment? You don't even want to know.

In the world of network marketing, the very idea of a glass ceiling for women is ludicrous. Your network marketing company doesn't care if you're female or male, black or white, a college grad or a high-school dropout. It only cares about how diligently and effectively you build your network—and as I pointed out, there are four times as many women as there are men doing exactly that.

The key is your skills, education, and experience. There are no limits and no ceilings, glass or otherwise, for women in the world of network marketing.

4) No Limits on Income

Because of the glass ceiling and the still-present wage inequality between men and women in the job market, a woman is often limited in the amount of income she can make. Studies show that women with the same education and experience as their male counterparts earn about seventy-four cents for every dollar their male peers earn.

But a network marketing business is *fully scalable*. Regardless of gender, in network marketing, the size of the income stream you can generate by building your network is without limit.

5) Increased Self-Esteem

Personally, I think this is one of the greatest benefits and rewards to a network marketing business—and it is one of the strongest reasons women become involved in the business. It's not unusual for a woman's self-esteem to be linked to her ability to provide for herself. Being dependent on anyone for your financial life can lead to a reduced sense of self-worth. You may do things you otherwise would not do if money were no issue.

I've seen women's self-esteem soar once they know how to make it on their own financially. And when a woman's self-esteem rises, the relationships around her tend to improve. Higher self-esteem leads to greater success, which ultimately leads to the greatest gift of all—freedom.

6) Control of Your Time

When it comes to devoting energy to building genuine wealth, one major impediment women often have far more than men is the simple matter of *time*. This is especially true for mothers who spend many hours taking care of children. I hear from many women, "After I come home from work, I have to get dinner ready, help my kids with their homework, and clean up the dishes. By the time everyone's in bed and I have a free moment to myself, I'm exhausted!"

As a network marketer, you are in control of your time. This business is something you can do part time or full time. It is something you can do from your home, on the phone and computer, in the evenings, weekends, anytime, anywhere. It is a business that can travel with you, that you can keep in your pocket, and that you can engage in half-hour increments, if that's what your schedule and circumstances dictate.

Wealth-Building Is a Necessity

These six reasons support why women so strongly need to learn how to build their own wealth. The statistics prove how much times have changed for women and point out that our need for real-life financial education is no longer a luxury; it's a necessity. Depending on someone else for your financial future is like rolling the dice. The reward may be there in the end, but the risk is steep.

Glass ceilings and limits to income are what so many women have been fighting against for ages. Both disappear in the world of network marketing. And then two of the greatest gifts of all—a higher sense of self-worth and time to spend exactly as you want—can be yours.

However, out of all these reasons I've just listed, I have no way of knowing which speaks the most to you. You are not the "average woman"; you are you. And the single most compelling reason for building your network marketing business is one that only you can determine.

Create Your Wealth ... and Have Fun Doing It

Regardless of what that compelling reason is, you have to remember one more thing when starting a network marketing business, and that is to *have fun*.

Yes, it's great to think that you can earn an extra $100, $1,000, or even $10,000 a month, and that you can avoid dependency and have control of your time, but if you are not having fun, it can quickly lead to that same rut many find themselves in out in the corporate world. Simply put, you have to be passionate about what you do; the lack of it will reflect in your bank account.

That's why I think *party plan* businesses—a type of network marketing business that revolves around in-home parties—are ideal for so many woman looking to start their own businesses. Party plan businesses are the perfect opportunity to spend time with family and friends in the comfort of your own home even while you are creating a social network that will allow you to build wealth—and have fun doing it.

An interesting fact about the party planning sector is that during turbulent economic times, it continues to fare well. In fact, this is one reason the network marketing industry as a whole is such a force to be reckoned with. Companies such as Vorwerk (JAFRA Cosmetics), Mary Kay, Tupperware, Scentsy, Partylite, Stampin' Up, Jewels by Park Lane, the Longaberger Company, and Southern Living at Home are among sixty-four direct selling companies with an annual global wholesale revenue of $100 million or more.

According to a September 2009 *Direct Selling News* report, Tastefully Simple, a party plan company offering specialty food items, saw sales rise by 5 percent in 2008, despite the recession. Another, Pampered Chef (which was purchased by billionaire

Warren Buffett in 2002) saw a 5 percent increase in recruiting during that same time period.

What's the message here? Party plan companies offer a low-risk, highly rewarding opportunity for any woman looking to take charge of her financial future. I recommend it for stay-at-home moms looking to join the ranks of new entrepreneurs, working women looking to supplement their paychecks, college students hoping to earn a few extra dollars—any woman who wants to give herself the opportunity to create wealth ... and have fun doing it.

Know What's Important

On our very first date, Robert asked me what I wanted to do with my life. I told him I wanted to run my own business someday. He said, "I can help you with that." Within a month, we had a business going together.

But he also started talking to me about larger things, too—about spirituality, and asking me about my life's purpose. This was in the 1980s, when people were workaholics and proud of it. By the '90s, people began taking a closer look at their lives and asking some harder questions. But it was really after 9/11 that people started saying, "Whoa, wait a minute. Why am I running around like a hamster on a wheel? What am I doing with my life? Where is it all going?"

I hear women all the time say they are too busy to get involved in a part-time home-based business. I tell them, "Here's the key to making your business successful: You have to look at your life, really look at it, and ask yourself, 'What is it that is so meaningful to me that I have to *have* it in my life?'"

What is important enough to you that you'll make the time and devote the effort to building a business that generates its own income, and then use that income to build wealth that will take care of you for the rest of your life? Because if you don't identify what that is, it's just not going to happen.

Freedom is different for everyone; success is different for everyone. It's personal, and it *should* be personal. Numbers are abstract; whether it's five thousand dollars or one million dollars, it doesn't really mean anything until you give it the meaning it has in your own life.

Early in our marriage, Robert and I were both passionately committed to being in business for ourselves, to not having other people tell us what to do, and to being in control of our own financial destinies. That was so important to us that we were willing to put up with just about any hardship to make it happen.

And it took years—really, about ten years.

At times, the stress of having no income was enormous. We had all sorts of friends who were telling us we were crazy, that we should just go get regular jobs with regular paychecks, but that was what we absolutely did not want to do.

Finally we decided we had to do something. Robert began teaching some courses. I went to a friend who had a clothing line and asked her to let me market her clothes. I went to hair salons and set up little mini-boutiques. There was no paycheck in it, no guarantees, only sales commissions—and in truth, I really made very little in commissions. But it got me out there, doing something.

I learned that this is the essence of being an entrepreneur: You have to *go out there and make things happen*. And the only way you are going to do that is if you know what is really, truly important to you, and you realize that the only way you are going to have that is to create it yourself.

PART THREE

Your Future Starts Now

*What it will take to get your successful
network marketing business started*

CHAPTER 18

Choose Wisely

So you've decided to do start your own network marketing business. Congratulations! Now you face a choice. There are several thousand network marketing companies in operation. Which one are you going to join? And how do you choose?

Newcomers to network marketing often make this choice by default, by simply signing up with the first opportunity to come along. Now, it may well be that the first company you hear about is a great company, and a wise choice for you. But it should be an informed, educated choice that you make with care. This is your future we're talking about.

So how do you choose? On what criteria do you base your decision?

"Our company has the best compensation plan—you can make great money here!"

When I was investigating different network marketing companies, I often heard this comment. The people anxious to show me their business opportunity would tell me stories of people making hundreds of thousands of dollars a month from their business. Because I have met people who really do make hundreds of thousands of dollars a month from their network marketing business, I don't doubt its massive earning potential.

Yet I do not recommend looking into a network marketing business primarily for the money.

"We have the best, most premium-quality products—products that have changed people's lives!"

I heard this a lot, too. Profound product benefits were probably the No. 2 reason for joining that people gave me, money being No. 1. And again, I didn't doubt it. While I heard plenty of exaggeration and outright hype, I also found truly great products, some of which I still consume or use today. In fact, exceptionally high-quality products tend to be one of the hallmarks of network marketing.

Yet products are also not the most important benefit.

Let me repeat that:

> When choosing a company to work with, the product is **not** the most important consideration.

CHAPTER 18: *Choose Wisely*

I stress this because most people assume that the product is the most important thing. It's not. Remember, you're not taking a job as a salesperson; you're going into business for yourself, and the business you are in is *network-building*. And when you start looking around at different companies, the question foremost in your mind needs to be, "Is this company going to help me learn how to become a master network-builder?"

The No. 1 reason I recommend network marketing is for its system of real-world business education and personal development.

A network marketing system is set up to make it possible for anyone to share in the wealth. It is open to anyone who has drive, determination, and perseverance. It does not care what your family name is or what college you went to (or if you went to one at all), how much money you make today, what race or sex you are, how good-looking you are, how popular you are, or even how smart you are.

Most network marketing companies care primarily about how much you are willing to learn, to change, and to grow, and whether you have the guts to stick it out through thick and thin while you learn to be a business owner.

Is this true of every single network marketing company out there? No. As in anything, there are the good, the bad, and the ugly—and there are also the truly great.

Not all network marketing companies really support education. There are some that are just about hustle: They just want you to go sell for them, and don't really care about teaching you anything. They just want you to bring your friends and family into the fold. If you run into one of those companies, I would be leery about getting involved: They won't contribute to your growth and may not be around long.

But the better companies out there will be totally dedicated to your business education. They are committed to the long haul and place a priority on developing your skills and your abilities. When you find a company like that, with leaders above you who are willing to train you and help you become the businessperson you can be, that's a company to stay with.

Is the compensation plan important? Sure. Is the quality of the product line critical? Of course. But far more than those things, what I really look at is how dedicated the company is to developing you as a strong B quadrant individual—a genuine wealth-building businessperson. That's the most important thing about the network marketing company you affiliate with: It really is your business school.

If you like what you hear from the initial presentation, take some time to actually meet the people who do the educating and training.

Invest the time to look past the compensation and products and really peer into the heart of the company: Is it truly interested in training and educating you? This takes more time than just listening to a thirty-minute sales pitch, clicking through a colorful Web site, and hearing about how much money people are making. To find out how good a company's education really is may require you to get off your couch and look into its training, educational seminars, and events.

If you like what you hear from the initial presentation, take some time to actually meet the people who do the educating and training.

And look carefully, because many network marketing companies say they have great educational plans, but not all do. In some companies I looked into, the only training they had was a recommended book list, and then they focused on training you to recruit your friends and family into the business.

So take your time and look carefully, because there *are* quite a few network marketing companies that do have excellent educational and training plans—in fact, some of the best real-life business training I've seen anywhere.

Here are a few questions to ask yourself about a network marketing company.

- Who's running the ship?
- Does the company offer a proven plan of action?
- Does the company embrace both business skills and personal development as a regular part of its educational and training programs?
- Does the company have a strong, high-quality, and highly marketable product line that you can be passionate about?

Who's Running the Ship?

Inexperienced people, who approach a new business with an E quadrant or S quadrant perspective, often look at a company's products, pay plan, or promotion to judge the strength of the company. I skip over all that and look directly at the *principals*—the people at the helm.

It's not that the product and pay plan and everything else aren't important. But no company is perfect. Problems always happen. If you have the right people running the ship, then whatever goes wrong, they'll fix it. In fact, if you have great people running the company, there's no problem they *can't* fix. But if you have the wrong people at the helm, then when problems happen, there's absolutely nothing you can do about it.

You can't judge a book by its cover; look beyond the promotional videos and Web sites. Look at the principals. What are their backgrounds, their experience, their track records, their character? Whether or not you get to know them personally or ever work with them directly, *they* are the partners you're getting into business with.

John: One thing I'd like to address here is the myth that eager promoters sometimes spread: that in order to make "the big money," you have to "get in on the ground floor." This is just not true.

CHAPTER 18: *Choose Wisely*

Robert: Not only is it not true, it's plain stupid! The majority of business startups fail within their first year or two, and that includes startup network marketing corporations. Why would you want to risk your hard work, time, and energy by investing all that in a company that doesn't yet have a track record?

John: There are strong, viable, excellent network marketing companies that are 3 years old, and there are those that are 30 years old. It's true that there is something exciting and invigorating about being part of something that is still young and in its fresh beginnings. But there is also a lot of power and credibility that comes with being affiliated with a company that has been in business for decades.

I would exercise due caution about committing yourself to a company that has barely opened its doors. Yet, even here, there are exceptions; you may find a new company that is just starting out, yet has such strong corporate credentials that it merits serious consideration.

The point here is, do your due diligence: Find out what it is you're looking at and who you're getting into business with.

Don't be fooled by people telling you that the trick to getting rich is being with a brand-new company, or a 5-year-old company, or a 35-year-old company. There is no "trick." There is no magic formula. What you want is a company that knows what it's doing and gives you clear signs that it's going to be there for the long haul.

Does the Company Offer a Proven Plan of Action?

John: The most lucrative and viable network marketing opportunities will not expect you to reinvent the wheel. Instead, they will offer plans of action to help you create the success you're after. For example, they will have a training guide with suggested daily or weekly activities.

Some companies will offer business owners a personalized Web site to help educate prospects or share products and opportunities. First-class, professional presentation tools such as CDs, DVDs, podcasts, and print materials have become standard fare for the typical network marketer's toolbox.

Does the Company Embrace Both Business Skills and Personal Development as a Regular Part of Its Educational and Training Programs?

I've made it pretty clear that I hold the training and education you get as the No. 1 value in your network marketing experience, even more than the income stream you're building. So make sure it's there.

Make sure your company places a high value on regular training, both in business skills and also in character development and personal growth. For decades, the leaders in this industry have known that it pays to provide their people a steady diet of great inspirational and educational material. In the old days, it was books and audiotapes. In the 21st century, it's CDs, DVDs, podcasts, live teleconferences, and webinars—and yes, books. Books never go out of style!

> **John:** And live events, too. Even in the Internet age, there is something powerful about being physically present at a live event, something that no other medium can fully replace.
>
> These days, the day-to-day business of building a network is typically conducted over the phone and the Internet as much as it is face to face. But you'll still find that the better companies put a strong focus on their annual, semiannual, quarterly, and/or monthly events. Why? For their educational, training, and personal-development value.
>
> And by the way, it's not just the network marketing corporation itself who will be involved in your training and education. You have a whole hierarchy of people—from the person who actually enrolls you directly into the business (often termed your "sponsor") through *their* sponsor and all the way up the chain of sponsorship (your "upline"), all the way to the corporate officers themselves—and they *all* have a vested interested in seeing you grow, learn, and succeed.

One of the beauties of the network marketing system is that it is set up to be the exact opposite of the dog-eat-dog corporate environment, where even your best friend may climb over you to get to the next rung on the ladder.

In network marketing, that kind of cutthroat competition doesn't happen, simply because your sponsor's and upline's success depends on your success. The people who profit from your growth *want* you to grow!

Does the Company Have a Strong, High-Quality, and Highly Marketable Product Line That You Can Be Passionate About?

Even if it isn't consideration No. 1, the company's product offering is critically important. Why? Because of one word: *buzz.*

Network marketing companies typically don't do a lot of mass-media advertising. You don't often see billboards or TV ads for these products. Why not? Because they use a completely different promotional model. Instead of putting their advertising budgets into expensive mass media, they put their advertising budget into people like you.

> **John:** The lifeblood of a growing network is word-of-mouth—individual people telling other people about their product or service and the opportunity they have become a part of.

Because of that, the products and services that typically do really well in the network marketing model are those that people get excited about, those that have a great story to them, those that have an intriguing ingredient or unique history, those that provide the user especially powerful benefits, or those that are the first of their kind—products or services that tell a unique story.

In a word: *buzz*.

Now, don't get me wrong: I'm not talking about hype. I'm talking about genuine qualities and attributes. Your product has to be the real deal.

That said, it's important to remember there is no one "best" product. There is room for thousands of best products and services. To some extent, choosing a great product is a highly subjective thing. Some people have a strong affinity for skincare products, say, or nutrition, or technology.

Is there a strong market for the product? Is it something that will appeal to vast numbers of people? Is it priced competitively?

Do you believe in the product's value, and will you use it personally? Does it have a great story to tell? When you are genuinely passionate about the product you're sharing with others, they'll be more likely to become excited about it, too.

CHAPTER 19

What It Takes

So what does it take to build your own successful network marketing business? First, let's look at what it *doesn't* take.

You Don't Need an MBA or High-Powered Business Background

Remember the word *duplicable*. The strategies that work best in networking are those that *duplicate* best. Network marketing does for a B quadrant business model what Henry Ford did for the automobile industry: It reduces the process to component parts that can be mass-produced.

John: A successful network marketing business is not a handcrafted masterpiece made by one skilled pair of hands. It's a symphony of simplicity crafted by hundreds of thousands of hands.

You Don't Have to Be "Great at Sales"

Again, one of the biggest misconceptions that people who are not actually in network marketing often have about the business is that you need to be a "born salesman" to be successful here.

Nothing could be further from the truth. In fact, holding onto that idea will hurt you in network marketing. Why? Because "great salesman" types cannot duplicate themselves.

John: Remember, this is not principally a sales business, but a teaching, team-building, and leadership business. Your job is not to sell a lot of product, and it isn't even to teach a lot of people to sell a lot of product. It's to lead, train, and build people. It is first and foremost to build a network.

Robert: *Making the sale* is not the point; *building the network* is the point.

John: Exactly.

CHAPTER 19: *What It Takes*

You Don't Need to Quit Your Job!

In fact, it's vastly preferable *not* to quit your job when you're starting out. For one thing, building your own business is not like starting a new job, where you start earning a paycheck the moment you show up for work. It's going to take time to build your network. Give it time.

> **John:** And not only for financial reasons. Even if you could afford to quit your job, many new networkers find that once they get their businesses going, being connected to their co-workers can serve as a source for prospective partners or referrals to prospective partners.

The great majority of network marketers build their businesses part-time. The 2008 National Salesforce Survey conducted by the Direct Selling Association showed that only about one in eight network marketers worked twenty hours or more per week on their business.

You Don't Need to Be Rich or Take out a Second Mortgage on Your Home

Most network marketing businesses require less than $500 in actual out-of-pocket startup costs. Make no mistake about it: What you save in cash capital you will make up for in sweat equity and passion. The major investment in most self-owned businesses is investment of *oneself*, in the form of time, focus, and persistence. But you don't need a pile of cash to start.

> **John:** Still, just because the capital investment is low does not mean it's nonexistent. This is a business, and you need to run it like a business. And that means you will have monthly operating costs.
>
> Typically, your monthly budget will be very modest: a monthly supply of the product sampling, and the cost of contact and presentation tools, such as those mentioned above (CDs, DVDs, Web sites, etc.), as well as ongoing business-development and personal-development materials.
>
> So, no, you don't need a big cash stake to start, but you *do* need to budget some reasonable monthly expenditures.

You Don't Need to Be a Genius at Negotiation or a Whiz at Numbers

You do need a burning desire and determination fueled by a strong dose of passion.

"You have to love what you do," says my friend Donald Trump. "Without passion, great success is hard to come by. As an entrepreneur, you'll have tough times if you aren't passionate about what you're doing."

Those are a few of the things it *doesn't* take to build a successful network marketing business. Now let's look at what it *does* take.

It Takes Being Honest with Yourself

Building a B quadrant business is not an easy task. You need to ask yourself, "Do I have what it takes? Am I willing to go beyond my comfort zone? Am I willing to be led as well as to learn to lead? Is there a rich person inside of me, ready to come out?" If the answer is "Yes," then start looking for a network marketing business that has a great training program.

> **John:** I would also add this: Make sure you are clear on where you are and what you would like to accomplish in your life. Having a vision for what you would like to accomplish is essential.
>
> Then, get clear on your expectations. Get clear on what it will take, in terms of time put in each week, as well as money, skills, and resources. Get clear on what actions you'll need to take to make this business successful. Get clear on a realistic time frame.

In the book I wrote with Donald Trump, *Why We Want You to Be Rich*, Donald wrote:

"Network marketing requires an entrepreneurial spirit, and that means focus and perseverance. I do not recommend network marketing to people who are not highly self-motivated."

Donald is absolutely right.

It Takes the Right Attitude

For me, becoming an entrepreneur is an ongoing process, one that I am still involved in. I believe I will be an entrepreneur-in-training till the end. I love business, and I love solving business problems. It is a process that brings me the kind of life I want. So, although the process has been tough for me at times, it has been worth it.

One thought has kept me going; it was my glow in the dark, even in the darkest of hours. I had a small piece of paper from a Chinese fortune cookie taped to the base of an office phone at our surfer wallet company that read:

> *You can always quit. Why start now?*

There were many phone calls that I had to handle that provided me with more than enough reasons to quit. Yet, after hanging up the phone, I would glance at the words of wisdom from the fortune cookie and say to myself, "As much as I want to quit, I won't quit today. I'll quit tomorrow."

The good thing is, tomorrow never came.

My rich dad used to say if getting rich were easy, everybody would be rich. That's why, when people ask what was the No. 1 thing that allowed me to become rich, I say that I didn't want anybody to tell me what to do. I wanted my freedom so badly. I didn't want job security. I wanted financial freedom. And that's what network marketing offers.

CHAPTER 19: *What It Takes*

If you like somebody telling you how much you can make and when you should arrive and leave work, then a network marketing business is not for you.

It Takes Real Growth

A network marketing business can be a B quadrant business. But that doesn't necessarily mean it *will* be. That's up to you.

Network marketing is the perfect vehicle for people who want to enter the world of the B quadrant. While your income potential in the E and S quadrants is typically limited to how much *you as an individual* can produce, in a network marketing business, you can earn as much as your network generates. That means, once you build a very large network, you can earn a massive amount of money.

However, simply joining a network marketing company does not make your new venture a B quadrant business—not until it's truly large.

John: The technical definition of a "big business" is one that encompasses 500 or more people. Again, those 500 are usually described as "employees," but the point is the numbers involved. When you build a network of 500 or more independent representatives, what you have definitely fits the definition of a *big*, or B quadrant, business. And a network marketing business system is designed to expand to well over 500 people. It's common for an individual's network organization to grow to several thousand or even tens of thousands, and it is not unusual to see network organizations of *hundreds* of thousands.

Newcomers to the networking business often make the mistake of treating their fledgling network's income as "free money"—readily disposable income from Day One. But when you have just 5, 10, 50, or even 100 or 200 people in your network, your new business is still very much in the formative period. It is not yet a *big* business.

Once your network grows beyond 500 people and is getting into the thousands, you have a true B quadrant business that is generating passive income. It is not only a viable network; it is an income-generating asset.

But this means that the interval from when you join your company up to the point that you reach that 500-plus scale of business is a formative period, a time of laying your foundation. Keep it in perspective. Keep your eye on the real goal: wealth-building.

It Takes Time

If you have the idea that you can start a network marketing business and expect to start making money right away, then you are still thinking like someone who lives in the E or S quadrants. In fact, it is people in the E and S quadrants who are most often sucked into the get-rich-quick schemes and scams of life.

John: There is no such thing as a get-rich-quick method in network marketing. While the activities of the business are simple, they require time and effort, the foundation of passive income.

The DSA says that, on average, one in ten contacts will say "yes" to the opportunity. However, that figure improves with the business owner's level of experience. Remember, this number will hold true in volume. Though you may not find it average for just 10 contacts, you'll discover it is true for 100 contacts.

Over the years, there have been some people who have promoted the network marketing business as a sort of "fast track" to wealth. Of course, this is total nonsense. The people in network marketing who have developed their leadership skills, built their businesses, and developed genuine wealth have spent long, hard years doing it.

So don't be fooled if you hear anyone try to tell you that you should see quick results. This isn't some sleight-of-hand or six-month, hit-it-lucky joyride: This is serious business. This is *your life* we're talking about here.

In the real world of business, if you cannot start producing business within three to six months, you are fired. Xerox was a little more generous: They gave me a year to learn and a year of probation. If I hadn't had those two years, I would have been fired.

Your situation is different: Your network marketing company is not going to fire you—so don't fire yourself. Don't give it a few months or a year of effort and then say, "Oh well, I guess that didn't work out." Give it the time it needs.

Robert: John, when I tell people, "Give it time," I invariably get the question, "Okay—how *much* time?" How would you answer that?

John: I say give it five years.

Robert: That's exactly the same answer I give! In fact, it's the same for building *any* kind of business—I call it "my five-year plan."

The Five-Year Plan

If you are serious about starting your journey, I recommend committing to a minimum of five years of learning, growing, changing your core values, and meeting new friends. Why? *Because that's realistic.*

It took years for Howard Schultz to build Starbucks, for Ray Kroc to build McDonald's, and for Michael Dell to build Dell Computers. It takes time to build great companies and great business leaders. It took me years to build my own successful B quadrant business. It will take you years to build your network marketing business. Why should it be any different?

Most people don't think in terms of years; trained by advertising and the paycheck-to-paycheck values of the E quadrant, they think in terms of immediate gratification. Is it any wonder that so many people, when they first consider putting their toe into the B world, are so susceptible to the idea of "get rich quick"?

"I signed up a week ago. When do I start making the big money?"

Folks, *get rich quick* is an oxymoron. A rich relationship doesn't happen quickly; a richly rewarding novel is never written overnight. Creating richness, by definition, takes time, and this is just as true of financial richness as it is of any other kind. This is why there are so few people in the B quadrant. Most people want money but are unwilling to invest their time.

Ten thousand hours: Do the math. If you work eight hours a day, five days a week, you hit the 10,000-hour mark after *five years* of full-time effort.

In his book *Outliers: The Story of Success*, Malcolm Gladwell explains that to become outstandingly accomplished at anything, it takes about 10,000 hours of hard work. As a high-school kid, Bill Gates put in 10,000 hours of programming. When they were still just another unknown British band of wannabes, the Beatles played a nightclub in Hamburg, seven hours a day, seven days a week—and put in about 10,000 hours.

"What's really interesting about this 10,000-hour rule," says Gladwell, "is that it applies virtually everywhere. You can't become a chess grandmaster unless you spend 10,000 hours on practice. The tennis prodigy who starts playing at 6 is playing in Wimbledon at 16 or 17 [like] Boris Becker. The classical musician who starts playing the violin at 4 is debuting at Carnegie Hall at 15 or so."

Ten thousand hours: Do the math. If you work eight hours a day, five days a week, you hit the 10,000-hour mark after *five years* of full-time effort.

Fortunately for you, mastering network marketing is not like becoming a chess grandmaster. You don't need to become Boris Becker, the Beatles, or Bill Gates. You don't need to become the best in the world—but you do have to master the skills of the business. It won't take you five years of full-time, forty-hour weeks. But to learn and master what it takes to build a massive network with passive income, do yourself a favor and give yourself enough time.

By the way, I *still* use this five-year plan.

When I decide to learn something new—for example, investing in real estate—I still allow myself five years to learn the process. When I wanted to learn how to invest in stocks, I again gave myself five years to learn the process. Many people invest once, lose a few dollars, and then quit. They quit after their first mistake, which is why they fail to learn. But losing is part of the process of winning. It's only losers who think that winners never lose, who think that mistakes must be avoided at all costs. Mistakes are priceless opportunities to learn essential lessons.

Today, I still give myself five years to make as many mistakes as possible. I do this because I know that the more mistakes I make and learn from, the smarter I will become. If I make no mistakes for five years, then I am no smarter than I was five years ago—just five years older.

Give Yourself Time to Unlearn, *Too*

As much learning as you'll do in this business, chances are good there is also a substantial amount of *unlearning* that needs to happen.

One reason so many people get so entrenched in the E and S quadrants is that they start to feel comfortable there. It isn't that these quadrants are inherently more comfortable. After all, you're being taxed like crazy, your time is never your own, you're often forced to work with people you can't stand … in so many ways these quadrants are really quite *uncomfortable*. But people start to *feel* comfortable there because they have spent years learning how to be there, and it's what they know.

That all changes when you enter the world of network marketing. The job experience that comes from time spent in traditional employment or self-employment is often not that useful in network marketing. Fixed work hours, set wages or salaries based on time put in, the structure of having bosses and management hierarchies, narrowly defined job descriptions, a clearly defined clientele, a clearly defined territory and physical plant—so many of the trappings of the conventional workplace simply don't exist in this business.

If you have worked in traditional sales, as we said before, you'll actually want to unlearn those skills to a good degree, because in network marketing, it's not what you can do that counts, it's what you can do *and duplicate*.

If you have experience managing employees, you'll need to do some unlearning there, too—because in network marketing, you don't hire, fire, or tell people what to do. It's an entirely new dynamic, this business of the 21st century, and to excel here, you will likely need to leave some old habits behind.

Take your time to unlearn as well as to learn. For some people, the hardest part of switching from the left side of the quadrant to the right side of the quadrant is to unlearn the point of view of the E and S quadrants. Once you have unlearned what you had learned, the change will go much faster and easier.

It All Comes Down to Action

You can plan all you want, study all you want, and learn all you want, but the only people who win in network marketing are people who take action—today, tomorrow, and every day.

CHAPTER 20

Living the Life

What makes you rich? Most people would answer, "Money, of course!" And they would be wrong. Having money does not make you rich, because you can always lose money. Owning real estate does not make you truly rich, because (as we have seen dramatically in the last few years) real estate can always lose value.

So what makes you rich? *Knowledge.*

My Golden Lesson

As a young adult, even before I began investing in real estate, my very first investment was in gold. "Gold is the only true money," I reasoned. "How could I go wrong?" I began buying gold coins in 1972, when gold was approximately $85 an ounce. I was 25 years old. By the time I was 32, gold was approaching $800 an ounce, and my money had multiplied nearly *tenfold*. Hot dog!

The frenzy was on, and greed overtook caution. Rumors were that gold was going to hit $2,500 an ounce. Greedy investors began piling on, even those who had never bought gold before. I could have sold my gold coins for a significant profit, but I hung on, hoping for gold to go higher. About a year later, with gold sagging back below $500 an ounce, I finally sold my last coin. I watched gold drift lower and lower until 1996, when it finally bottomed at $275 in 1996.

It is not real estate, gold, stocks, hard work, or money that makes you rich; it is *what you know* about real estate, gold, stocks, hard work, and money that makes you rich. Ultimately, it is your *financial intelligence* that makes you rich.

I didn't make much money with it, but gold taught me a priceless lesson about money. Once I saw that I could actually *lose* money investing in "real money,"

CHAPTER 20: *Living the Life*

I realized that it was not the tangible asset that was valuable. It was *information* relative to the asset that ultimately made a person rich or poor.

It is not real estate, gold, stocks, hard work, or money that makes you rich; it is *what you know* about real estate, gold, stocks, hard work, and money that makes you rich. Ultimately, it is your *financial intelligence* that makes you rich.

Financial intelligence has little or nothing to do with academic intelligence. You can be a genius when it comes to academic intelligence, but a moron when it comes to financial intelligence.

1) Knowing How to Make More Money

The more money you make, the higher your financial intelligence. Someone who earns a $1 million a year has a higher financial IQ than one who earns $30,000 a year.

2) Knowing How to Protect Your Money

The world is out to take your money, and it's not just the Bernie Madoffs. One of the biggest financial predators is your government, who takes your money *legally*.

Take two people who both make $1 million a year. If one pays 20 percent in taxes while the other pays 35 percent, the first person has a higher financial IQ.

3) Knowing How to Budget Your Money

Many people fail to keep much money out of what they earn, simply because they budget like a poor person rather than like a rich person. Budgeting your money also takes financial intelligence.

Take two people: Person A earns $120,000 a year, and Person B earns only $60,000 a year. Who has more financial intelligence, Person A? Not so fast. Let's say Person A also *spends* $120,000 every year, putting him at Square 1 at year's end. But Person B, who earns only $60,000, budgets carefully and is able to live well on just $50,000, and invests the remaining $10,000. Who ends up with more?

If you have poor money-management skills, then all the money in the world cannot save you. If you budget your money wisely, and learn about the B and I quadrants, then you are on the path to great personal fortune and, most importantly, freedom.

Being able to live well and still invest *no matter how much or how little you make* requires a high level of financial intelligence. Having a surplus is something you have to actively budget for.

4) Knowing How to Leverage Your Money

After you budget a surplus, the next financial challenge is to leverage that surplus. Return on investment is yet one more measurement of financial intelligence.

The person who earns 50 percent on his money has a higher financial IQ than one who earns 5 percent. And the one who earns 50 percent *tax-free* on his money has a much higher financial IQ than the one who earns just 5 percent and then pays 35 percent in taxes on that 5 percent return!

Most people save their financial surplus, if they have any, by sticking it in a bank or putting it into a mutual fund portfolio, hoping this will leverage their money. But there are much better ways to leverage your money than savings and mutual funds. Those don't require much financial intelligence: You can train a monkey to save money and invest in mutual funds—which is exactly why the returns on those investment vehicles are historically pretty pitiful.

A Magnificent Life

The purpose of your network marketing business is not simply to make you money, but to give you the skills and financial intelligence so that you will use that additional money to build genuine wealth.

But even that is not the end goal. The end goal of building that wealth is so that you can live a magnificent life.

From my observations of people in many different situations, I would say there are three ways to live. These three ways are driven by three different emotions, and also correspond closely to three different financial and emotional states:

LIVING IN FEAR

I know what it's like to be broke. I've described how, in 1985, in many ways the worst year of my life, Kim and I were in such dire straits financially that we were literally homeless and living in our old broken-down Toyota. The feeling of fear during those days was paralyzing, so intense that it numbed our entire bodies.

I knew this feeling: It was the same sense I had as a young child, growing up in a family that was broke most of the time. That dark cloud of "not enough money" hung over our family for most of my childhood. Not having enough money to live on is a horrible experience, and it hurts in many more ways than financial. It can undermine your self-confidence and sense of self-worth, and sabotage every aspect of your life.

LIVING IN ANGER AND FRUSTRATION

The second way of living is living with the emotion of anger or frustration from having to get up and go to work, especially when you would rather be doing something else. A person who lives with this feeling may be someone who has a good job and high pay but cannot afford to stop working. That is where the frustration comes from. They know if they stop, the world they live in would come crashing down.

People like this may say, "I cannot afford to quit. If I quit, the banks would come and take everything away." These people often say, "I can't wait until my next vacation," or "Only ten more years to retirement."

CHAPTER 20: *Living the Life*

LIVING IN JOY, PEACE, AND CONTENTMENT

The third way of living is to live with the peace of mind of knowing that, regardless of whether you work or not, there is plenty of money coming in. This is the feeling Kim and I have lived with ever since 1994, when we sold our business and retired. Kim was then 37 and I was 47. Today, many years later, we still work; in fact, we work *hard*. Why? Because we love what we do.

The feeling of not *having* to work, knowing that no matter what we do we'll have more than enough money coming in for as long as we live, is an amazingly freeing, exhilarating feeling, allowing us to do what we genuinely love.

We spend our time together, and whether we're playing golf, traveling around the world, or putting in long hours in our boardroom, to us, it's all play and it's all the stuff of dreams. It's our life, exactly as we've always wanted it to be, and we treasure every single moment of it.

Ants, Grasshoppers, and Human Beings

Earlier I mentioned the fable of the ant and the grasshopper. We all grew up with this idea that there are two ways to live: You can live like the good, modest, industrious, and frugal ant and sock away crumbs for the future, or, like the irresponsible and spendthrift grasshopper, dance and fiddle away the days without a thought of the future.

In some ways, this image has done us more harm than good. Sure, it's good to be responsible and frugal, and to prepare for the future. But look at the ant's lifestyle! Do you really want to be a cog in a gigantic ant colony, pushing little crumbs of dirt around, day after day, for the rest of your life?

Let's face: We're not ants, and we're not grasshoppers, either; we're *human beings*. Is it unreasonable to expect that we should be able to live the full lives which we humans are capable of living?

If you grasp the basics of wealth; if you manage your money, your time, and your attention with intelligence; if you create big dreams and have the audacity to follow them; then you *can* live a life that meets with a success unexpected in common hours.

CHAPTER 21

The Business of the 21st Century

One reason I have such strong respect for network marketing is that it is a genuine equal-opportunity business. Network marketing casts a very wide net. When you look closely at the more than sixty million people worldwide who are engaged in the business, you'll find people of every color and creed, every age group, and every level of background, experience, and skill.

This also makes it the business of the future. In the 21st century, we are realizing as never before that wealth, as I said earlier, is not a zero-sum game. It's not a question of some of us prospering by holding others down. The future of genuine wealth lies in pioneering ways of doing business that elevate the financial well-being of humanity.

Those are my personal business values, and network marketing shares those values. And championing those values not only *feels* good—it's also *good business*.

Democratic Wealth-Building

One of the principal reasons I have put so much energy into supporting and promoting the network marketing industry is simply this: Its systems are fairer than previous systems of acquiring wealth.

A network marketing system is set up to make it possible for anyone to share in the wealth. This is a very democratic way of wealth creation. The system is open to anyone who has drive, determination, and perseverance. The system does not really care what college you went to or whether you went to one at all. It does not care how much money you are making today, what race or sex you are, how good-looking you are, who your parents are, or how popular you are. Most network marketing companies care primarily about how much you are willing to learn, to change and to grow, and whether you have the guts to stick it out through thick and thin while you learn to be a business owner.

Network marketing is more than just a good idea; in many ways, it is the business model of the future. Why? Because the world is finally starting to awaken to the reality that the Industrial Age is over.

Chapter 21: *The Business of the 21st Century*

For a world with less and less of its former security, network marketing is emerging as a new engine of individual achievement and security. Network marketing gives millions of people throughout the world the opportunity to take control of their lives and their financial futures. That is why, even though Old World thinkers persist in not seeing it yet, the network marketing industry will continue to grow.

In the years ahead, I expect to see an explosion in the prevalence, penetration, visibility, and maturation of leading network marketing companies.

Earlier I wrote about how Thomas Edison became rich, not by making a better light bulb, but by creating the network that supported the light bulb. Edison had a young employee named Henry who did something very similar with another new invention that, at the time, seemed to have no real practical use.

> **By its very nature and design, network marketing is a strikingly fair, democratic, socially responsible system of generating wealth.**

Like Edison with the light bulb, young Henry Ford did not invent the automobile, but he did something radical that forever changed the invention's destiny, along with the destiny of millions of people. At the turn of the century, the automobile was seen as a curiosity, a rich person's toy. And indeed, they were so inordinately expensive that only the rich could afford to own one. Ford's radical idea was to make the automobile available to *everyone*.

By slashing production costs and adapting the assembly line to mass-produce standardized inexpensive cars, Ford became the largest automobile producer in the world. Not only did he make his car affordable, he also paid the highest wages in the industry and even offered profit-sharing plans, redistributing over $30 million annually to his workers—and $30 million was worth a lot more in the early 1900s than it is today!

Ford's mission statement was to "Democratize the automobile," and in the course of fulfilling that mission, he made himself a very rich man.

Network marketing is a revolutionary form of business: For the first time in history, it is now possible for anyone and everyone to share in the wealth that, until now, has been reserved only for the chosen few or the lucky.

The business is not without its detractors. And it has had its share of hucksters and flim-flam artists, unethical people trying to make a quick buck. But by its very nature and design, network marketing is a strikingly fair, democratic, socially responsible system of generating wealth.

Despite what its detractors will tell you, network marketing is not a very good business for greedy people. In fact, the only way you can become rich in network marketing is by helping others become rich in the process. To me, this is as revolutionary as Thomas Edison and Henry Ford were in their day. By design, it is the perfect business for people who like helping other people.

I don't necessarily condemn greed; a little greed and personal self-interest are always healthy. But when the goal of personal gain grows out of perspective and people pursue it at the expense of others, it becomes repugnant. I believe that most people are inherently generous, and that we gain the greatest satisfaction and fulfillment from our own achievements when they also serve to lift up others, and not to keep them down.

Network marketing satisfies this generous impulse. It offers a path to personal success, to building great wealth and creating financial freedom through a process that operates successfully only through helping our fellow human beings.

You can become rich by being cheap and greedy. You can also become rich by being abundant and generous. The method you choose will be the method that most closely matches the core values deep inside of you.

An Economic Foundation for Peace

I flew helicopter missions over the jungles of Vietnam, and I know from firsthand experience what war is like. I also know that inequity is one of the core causes of war. As long as the gap between the rich and the poor widens, it is going to be tough to create conditions of peace. We can march for peace, give speeches endorsing peace, form committees to study peace, and promote peace, but it's going to be impossible to actually *create* that peace we talk about unless and until we can begin to bring substantially more economic opportunity to many millions of people.

And as huge a goal as that sounds, that is exactly what network marketing is doing.

Today, many network marketing companies are spreading peace through economic opportunity all over the world. Not only are network marketing companies thriving in all the major capitals of the world, but many are also working in developing nations, bringing financial hope to millions of people who live in impoverished countries. Most traditional corporations can only survive where people are rich and have money to spend.

It is time that people all over the world had an equal opportunity to enjoy a rich and abundant life, rather than spend their lives working hard only to make the rich richer.

It's time *you* had that opportunity.

Welcome to the 21st century.

ROBERT T. KIYOSAKI
Investor, Entrepreneur, Financial Education Advocate, and Best-Selling Author

Robert Kiyosaki is the author of *Rich Dad Poor Dad*—the No. 1 personal finance book of all time—a book that challenged and changed the way tens of millions of people think about money. *Rich Dad Poor Dad* ranks as the longest-running best-seller on all four of the lists that report to *Publisher's Weekly*—*The New York Times*, *Business Week*, *The Wall Street Journal*, and *USA Today*—and was named "*USA Today*'s No. 1 Money Book" two years in a row. It is the third-longest-running "how-to" best-seller of all time.

With perspectives on money and investing that often contradict conventional wisdom, Robert has earned a reputation for straight talk, irreverence, and courage. His point of view that the "old" advice—get a good job, save money, get out of debt, invest for the long term in a diversified portfolio of stocks, bonds, and mutual funds—is "bad" (both obsolete and flawed) advice, challenges the status quo. His assertion that "your house is not an asset" stirred controversy, but has been proven to be accurate for many homeowners.

Other *Rich Dad* titles hold four of the top ten spots on Nielsen Bookscan List's life-to-date sales from 2001–2008. Translated into fifty-one languages and available in 109 countries, the *Rich Dad* series has sold over 28 million copies worldwide and has dominated best-seller lists across Asia, Australia, South America, Mexico, and Europe. In 2005, Robert was inducted into the Amazon.com Hall of Fame as one of that bookseller's top twenty-five authors. There are currently twenty-seven books in the *Rich Dad* series. Among the notable titles is *Why We Want You to Be Rich: Two Men—One Message*, a book written with Robert's good friend Donald Trump in 2006 that debuted at No. 1 on the *New York Times* best-seller list. Already, the two friends and business giants are at work on a second book to be published in 2010.

Robert's latest books include *The Real Book of Real Estate*, a compilation of real-life lessons and advice from veteran real estate investors and advisors to Robert, and *Conspiracy of the Rich: The 8 New Rules of Money*, an innovative and groundbreaking free interactive online book that has garnered an unbelievable amount of unique visits and climbed as high as No. 5 on the *New York Times* how-to tradepaper best-seller list.

Robert has been featured on shows such as *Larry King Live* and *Oprah*, and was recently featured in *TIME* magazine's "10 Questions" column, a notable Q&A column that has featured such names as director Spike Lee and actor Michael J. Fox, among others.

In addition to his books, Robert writes a column—"Why the Rich Are Getting Richer"—for Yahoo! Finance and a monthly column titled "Rich Returns" for *Entrepreneur* magazine.

John Fleming

John Fleming was born and raised in Richmond, Virginia. His interest in architecture and desire to build was borne of a family tradition that dated back to his great-great-grandparents. A gifted student, his natural talent for architectural design flourished at the Illinois Institute of Technology, known for its adherence to the principles of Mies van der Rohe, one of the most renowned architects of modern times. Upon graduation, John worked for the great architect and was selected to do many of the illustrations in *Mies van der Rohe: The Art of Structure*, the last book published on him.

John's knowledge of and interest in architecture eventually led to the realization that the same principles of design and construction could be applied to life as well. These thoughts formed the foundation of his passionate belief that ordinary people could accomplish extraordinary things by following similar building concepts. It was this belief that led to his shift from the study of architecture to a career in direct selling.

John's decision to embrace the direct selling industry was guided by the knowledge that the industry had welcomed people from all walks of life—regardless of past experience or inexperience—for more than 100 years. He believed it enabled those willing to learn a few basic skills about selling and servicing others the opportunity to engage in the American free enterprise system. For the next 40 years, he tested his theories not only upon himself, but also upon thousands of others whom he believed could become the architects of their own destinies.

John has built a successful career as an entrepreneur, consultant, writer, and speaker. He has owned and operated his own direct selling company, served as an independent contractor, and held various executive positions with leading companies, including 15 years at Avon Products, Inc., where he led the company's western business unit in both top- and bottom-line growth for a record six consecutive years. John retired from Avon in 2005.

John has had a longtime affiliation with the Direct Selling Association and the Direct Selling Education Foundation, and currently serves as a board member for both organizations. In 1997, the Direct Selling Education Foundation recognized his contributions with its highest honor, the Circle of Honor Award.

Over the past several years, John has continued to create several organizational structures through which his consulting and leadership remain focused on business, educational, and life solutions. In 2006, he assumed the publisher and editor in chief duties of *Direct Selling News*, the trade publication serving the direct selling industry, where he now brings his knowledge and insight to industry leaders (www.directsellingnews.com). Since 2008, he has served as the executive director of the SUCCESS Foundation, a nonprofit organization dedicated to helping teens learn critical personal-development skills so they can achieve their full potential (www.SUCCESSFoundation.org). John is also the author of *The One Course*, which provides instruction on how to build a successful life using the principles of architecture (www.theonecourse.com).

KIM KIYOSAKI

With a passion for educating women about money and investing, Kim Kiyosaki draws on a lifetime of experience in business, real estate, and investing in her mission to support financial education. Kim has been a featured guest on *The Larry King Show*, FOX News, and *A BraveHeart View* Internet Television show, and she is the host of the PBS *Rich Woman* show. Kim was recently featured as a financial education advocate in *Essence* magazine, and she is a columnist for WomanEntrepreneur.com.

Kim is a self-made millionaire and a happily married (but fiercely independent) woman. Her first book, *Rich Woman: A Book on Investing for Women*, hit the *Business Week* best-seller list the month it was released. *Rich Woman* is a best-seller in numerous countries throughout the world, including Mexico, South Africa, India, Australia, New Zealand, and across Europe. Donald Trump stated about *Rich Woman*, "This book is a must-read for all women. Today, more than ever, women need to be financially savvy." *Rich Woman* was also listed on Donald Trump's Summer Reading List for 2009.

Kim has used the international forum of Rich Woman to showcase the startling statistics related to women and money, and through www.richwoman.com, she has created an interactive online community where women can learn and grow.

Kim Kiyosaki, and her husband Robert Kiyosaki, both know what it is like to be in the financial crisis situation that many Americans are confronting today. In the 1980s they were homeless, jobless, and over $400,000.00 in debt. At that difficult time, they created and followed a straightforward 10-step formula to get out of bad debt. They share that formula in the popular *How We Got Out of Bad Debt* audio CD. Today, they are successful entrepreneurs and best-selling authors.

In addition, Robert and Kim Kiyosaki created the CASHFLOW board game in 1996 to teach the financial and investment strategies that his rich dad spent years teaching him. It was those same strategies that allowed them to retire early. Today there are thousands of CASHFLOW Clubs throughout the world.

In 1997, Kim and Robert founded The Rich Dad Company. The company has launched the Rich Dad® message and mission of financial literacy—through books, games, and other educational tools—to international recognition and acclaim.

"Too many women, especially as we get older, are finding ourselves in dire financial straights—due to divorce, death of a spouse, or simply no planning. The problem is that so many of us have not been educated about money and investing. Financial education is not about how to buy car insurance or save pennies at the grocery store. I think we women are a little smarter than that. Women need to take control of our financial lives, instead of crossing our fingers hoping that someone else is looking out for our financial futures."

The Best-Selling Personal Finance Book of All Time!

Read the book that started it all, Rich Dad Poor Dad, *The New York Times* No. 1 best-seller six years running that changed how the world views money and investing.

Rich Dad Poor Dad teaches you to think like the rich, and explains how money works.

You learn:

- The importance of your personal financial statement and how to read one
- The difference between an asset and a liability
- How the middle class and the rich think differently about money
- Why to invest for cash flow instead of capital gains
- And much more!

*Robert Kiyosaki
Investor, Entrepreneur,
Educator, and Author*

Start your financial education today with Robert Kiyosaki's **Rich Dad Poor Dad,** the best-selling personal finance book of all time!

Order your copy at *richdad.com* today!

RICH DAD
knowledge: the new money

Bring Out the Rich Woman in You.

Rich Woman
Take Charge of Your Money. Take Charge of Your life!

Let's face it. When it comes to money, men and women are different. There are unique issues that women face when it comes to money and investing. And now there is a book on money uniquely for woman.

Now is the time for women to get smarter with their money. Kim Kiyosaki's passion is to educate and encourage women to create the financial security and peace of mind. That's why she wrote **Rich Woman.**

- Stop losing sleep over money
- Take control of your financial future
- Forget about looking for a rich Prince Charming
- Demand true independence

Start your journey to financial independence today.

"This book is a must-read for all women. Today, more than ever, women need to be financially savvy."
—Donald Trump

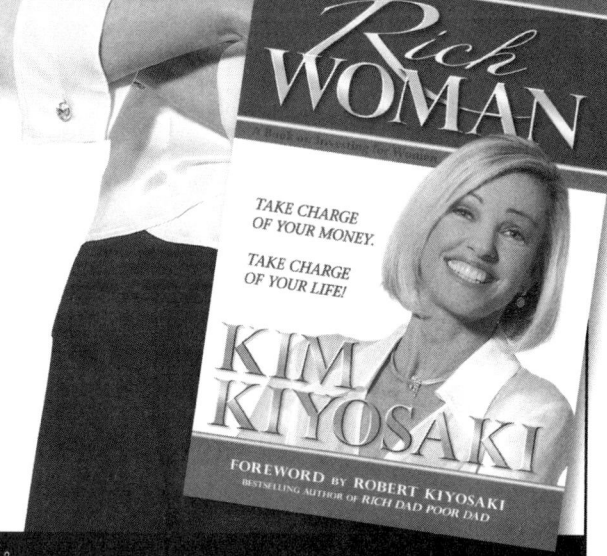

Get your copy of *Rich Woman* **Today!**

Order your copy at **richwoman.com**

The Board Game *USA Today* Calls Monopoly® on Steroids!

Leading researchers teach that we only retain 10% of what we read, but 90% of what we experience.

CASHFLOW 101, developed by Robert Kiyosaki, author of the #1 personal finance book of all time, **Rich Dad Poor Dad,** is an educational board game that simulates real life financial strategies and creates an experience that teaches you how to get out of the Rat Race and onto the Fast Track, how to make your money work for you – not the other way around.

- Practice real world investing with play money
- Learn the differences between an asset and a liability
- Discover the power of understanding your personal financial statement

Robert Kiyosaki
Investor, Entrepreneur,
Educator and Author

Experience CASHFLOW 101 Today!

Order your copy at *richdad.com* today!

RICH DAD
knowledge: the new money

CASHFLOW® CLUBS
Bring Out The Financial Genius In You!

Discover your financial genius. Join an official Rich Dad **CASHFLOW Club** today, and start your journey for a better tomorrow.

No matter which path you take to a rich life, there is a **CASHFLOW Club** to help guide you along the way. Play the **CASHFLOW Game**, called "Monopoly on steroids" by *USA Today*, in a highly interactive and unforgettably exciting environment.

- Learn to have your money work for you
- Distinguish between good and bad investments
- Complete the **CASHFLOW Club** 10-steps to increase your financial IQ
- Apply CASHFLOW Game's lessons to your life

By joining a **CASHFLOW Club** and completing the 10-steps to increase your financial IQ, you will see a new world, a world of Rich Dad, a world few people see!

Find your Official Rich Dad CASHFLOW Club today at **richdad.com**!

Is There A Conspiracy Against Your Wealth?

The First Rich Dad Book Written *Entirely Online* While History Was Being Made During the Worldwide Financial Crisis

Read the ground-breaking interactive book, Robert Kiyosaki's best-selling, **Conspiracy of the Rich,** and learn how the ultra-rich steal your wealth through taxes, debt, inflation, and retirement – and what you can do about it.

Spanning history, current events, and future trends, **Conspiracy of the Rich** was written and published online during the worst economic crises since the Great Depression, and includes reader comments and a bonus Q&A chapter.

- Learn about the conspiracy against financial education
- Discover why the dollar is doomed
- Gain the power to take charge of your own destiny

Don't miss one of the most talked about Rich Dad books of all time.

Order your copy of Rich Dad's Conspiracy of The Rich today!

Robert Kiyosaki
Investor, Entrepreneur,
Educator and Author

Order your copy at **richdad.com** today!

RICH DAD.
knowledge: the new money

A Wall Street Journal Best-seller, Robert Kiyosaki's CASHFLOW

Tired of Living Paycheck to Paycheck?

In the **CASHFLOW Quadrant,** the sequel to Robert Kiyosaki's smash hit, **Rich Dad Poor Dad,** you learn how the role you play in the world of money affects your ability to become financially free.

Learn the four types of people who make up the world of business:

- Employees
- Self-Employed
- Business owners
- Investors

And how you can move from being an employee or self-employed to capturing the power of being a business owner and investor.

The CASHFLOW Quadrant is the perfect guide to getting out of the Rat Race and onto the Fast Track.

Visit **richdad.com** and order your copy today!

Want To Be An Entrepreneur?

Entrepreneurship is on the rise, but there are only a handful of people who will be really successful. The dividing line between a successful entrepreneur and a struggling entrepreneur is financial knowledge.

In **Rich Dad's Before You Quit Your Job,** Robert Kiyosaki shares his successes, and more importantly, his failures – and the lessons they taught him.

- Think like a business owner and investor
- Discover the power of the B-I Triangle
- Build a firm foundation for future success

If you want to be an entrepreneur, this book will give you a jump-start to be successful and equip you with the tools you need to make your business thrive.

Jump-start your business today!

Order your copy at *richdad.com* today!

RICH DAD.
knowledge: the new money

Protect Your Teens Financial Future

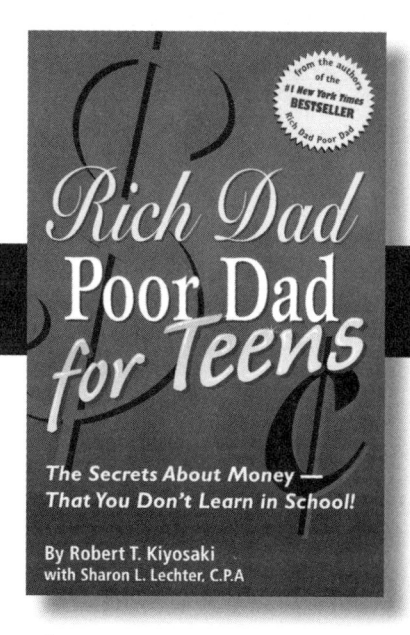

The school system is preparing your children for financial hardship and bad financial decisions due to a lack of financial education.

Picking up where school leaves off, **Rich Dad Poor Dad for Teens** is the secret weapon for teaching your child the way to gain freedom, to create wealth, and to understand how money works.

The book:
- Teaches teens how to make wise financial choices
- Uses fun tips, quizzes, sidebars to teach lessons with straight talk
- Helps jump-start your child's personal success

If you are concerned about your child's financial future, you can't afford to pass over this essential book for your teen.

Purchase your copy online at **richdad.com**

Rich Dad® Events
Books Are Just the Beginning

Tap into a style of learning that is proven more effective than reading. Move beyond the *Rich Dad* books and gain access to some of the best experts in the financial world at Rich Dad events.

- Highly interactive
- Simulate real life situations through financial games
- Practically apply Rich Dad principles
- Achieve your goals

According to the Cone of Learning we only retain 10% of what we read, but 70% to 90% of what we discuss and simulate. *Rich Dad* events are designed to help you experience maximum retention of *Rich Dad* concepts – and to help you apply them in real life.

There is always something happening in the world of Rich Dad!

Find your Official **Rich Dad** Event nearest you today at **richdad.com**!

BE THE ARCHITECT OF YOUR OWN DESTINY!
The One Course

Created by successful executive and entrepreneur John Fleming, *The One Course* is designed to guide you through the steps necessary for creating a successful life. It helps you identify the areas of your life that need designing, or redefining, and helps you "construct" a solid framework for the future that will allow you to live the life you truly want to live.

Each lesson features a summary that provides a high-level overview of the material. In addition, each summary includes a building principle that highlights an important phase or process needed in your personal development. Important lessons include:

- Creating the Vision
- Preparing the Plan
- Building Your Team
- Laying the Foundation
- Construction Phase
- Project Management

The 16 activities in *The One Course* serve as aids in identifying how to improve your overall plan. They consist of assessments that help you evaluate your goals, reflective journals that help you develop an awareness of where you are in life and where you want to be, and activities to strengthen practical skills.

Learn the principles for building a successful life today!

"Like the architecture it speaks of, The One Course is a work of art. The 14 building principles that John applies to everyday experiences are sure to help you lead an inspiring and exceptional life."
—Jim Rohn

Includes:
- 208-page workbook with exercises
- Audio version on 6 CDs
- Earl Nightingale's *The Strangest Secret* CD
- BONUS: *The One Course* Journal

Get Your Copy of *The One Course* **Today!**

Order your copy at **theonecourse.com**

Ideal Prospecting Tools
for Building Your Direct Selling Business!

The Business of the 21st Century *Book*

This is the definitive book for helping you get started in a network marketing business! In *The Business of the 21st Century*, Robert Kiyosaki shows you that while these may be economic hard times for the majority, for some entrepreneurs, they are times ripe with economic potential. Perfect for recruiting and distributor training. *142-page paperback book.*

The Perfect Business? *Audio*

In the exclusive audio interview, Robert Kiyosaki reveals his choice for the perfect business to help you retire rich. Prospects will discover successful strategies to create personal security and financial freedom. Excellent for recruiting! *Approximately 20 minutes.*

The Perfect Business! *Video*

Let Robert Kiyosaki show your prospects how direct selling can be their ticket to financial freedom. This exclusive video, shot in Robert's home, envelopes prospects with his revolutionary CASHFLOW Quadrant® wisdom, just as his rich dad shared it with him. Excellent for recruiting and follow-up. *Approximately 11 minutes.*

The Business School *Book*

With *The Business School for People Who Like Helping People* book, Robert Kiyosaki helps you build your network. Learn the Eight Hidden Values of a Network Marketing Business—Other Than Making Money! Robert reveals one of the quickest ways to build a B quadrant business and why the word *network* is so powerful to the rich. Excellent for recruiting and distributor training. *144-page paperback book.*

To order any of these products, check with your organization's tool supplier.